THE CONSCIENCE OF SERGEANT CLUFF

THE CONSCIENCE OF SERGEANT CLUFF

by

Leslie Sands

Warner Chappell Plays

LONDON

A Time Warner Company

First published 1991 by
Warner Chappell Plays Ltd.,
129 Park Street, London W1Y 3FA

© Copyright 1990 Leslie Sands

ISBN 0 85676 145 1

Printed by Commercial Colour Press, London E7.

CHARACTERS

Kathleen Norton
Ritchie
Cluff
Doctor Hewitt
Nell Norton
Annie Croft
Det. Sgt. David Barker
Inspector Mole
and
Clive, a black-and-white sheepdog.

The play is set in the living-kitchen at Daneghyll, a lonely farmstead in the heart of the Yorkshire Dales, not long ago.

ACT ONE

Scene One: An evening in September.
Scene Two: The next morning.

ACT TWO

Scene One: Shortly afterwards.
Scene Two: That evening.

ACT ONE

Scene One

The living-kitchen at Daneghyll Farm, in the heart of the Yorkshire Dales.

An evening in September.

The blind above the window is not yet lowered and the casement is a few inches open on its retaining-bar. The daylight outside is waning and the evening will be overcast. The old grandfather clock shows something after six p.m. A flurry of rain spatters the window now and again. The whole room is dim and lowering, the fire in the grate sullen.

Footsteps run across the yard outside before the door ULC *flies open and* KATHLEEN NORTON *enters, breathless and frightened. She slams the door shut behind her, and leans back against it.*

KATHLEEN is a country girl in her early twenties, frail-looking and younger than her years. She carries two parcels.

KATH   (*rooted*) Mother?

        (*No answer. She feels for the switch and switches on the ceiling light.*)

        (*again*) Mother!

        (*Silence still. She crosses to dump her parcels on the table, glancing nervously over her shoulder. She unbuttons her coat and feels in her pockets for loose change, which she places down beside the parcels. Then she crosses to the hearth, pulling off her damp headgear. As she starts to remove her weatherproof, the door to the hall* DR (*to which she has her back*) *is softly opened.* RITCHIE *steps through, quietly and unobserved, and stands just inside the room, his eyes roving her nubile figure wolfishly. He is her cousin, a general helper on his uncle's farm, and of roughly the same age as* KATHLEEN. *Everything about* RITCHIE *seems soiled and unclean. He is a countrified tearaway.*)

RITCHIE   (*grinning*) You needn't have bothered, lovey —

       (KATHLEEN *whirls, her coat in her hands, as he strolls towards her.*)

       Thought you'd dodge past the mistal, did you? Thought you'd dodge *me*? Fat chance!

KATH   (*backing slowly*) You wouldn't dare come in at the front, not if my mother was about —

RITCHIE   She isn't.

KATH   She'll know ... dragging your dirt all over the house —

RITCHIE   (*jeering*) I'm terrified!

       (*A beat, as they eye one another.*)

KATH   You haven't got my father round here now, to back you up.

RITCHIE   Don't be too sure. They haven't buried him yet.

KATH   They will tomorrow.

RITCHIE   She doesn't waste time — that mother of yours. Two days! (*As she flashes him a look.*) Don't shiver: dead men tell no tales. (*He starts forward.*)

KATH   Don't come any closer —

RITCHIE   (*stops*) How was it, down in Gunnarshaw? Folk, I mean. Did you find 'em sorry for you — or looking sideways, everyone you passed — telling tales?

KATH   Why don't you get back to your milking?

RITCHIE   Nowt to milk. Not till she brings 'em down.

       (*He reaches out to touch her, and she moves quickly out of his way.*)

RITCHIE | Tuppence to talk to you now, is it? Well, there's no hurry, far as I'm concerned. But if you know which side your bread's buttered —

KATH | Are you threatening me?

RITCHIE | Would I do a thing like that? We're all in it together, after all. (*Points towards ceiling.*) Ted was your father, but he was my uncle. Up to us now to keep the farm in the family. What you worried about? I'd do right by you.

KATH | Marry?

RITCHIE | We've known each other seven years —

KATH | And nothing but trouble since the day you came. Turning my father against my mother —

RITCHIE | (*easily*) No need was there, the way they felt about each other? Everybody knew, you know, down in Gunnarshaw. Ted knew, an' all — and he never did get used to playing second fiddle.

KATH | To what?

RITCHIE | Aw, come off it!

KATH | Show some respect! My father's lying dead upstairs —

RITCHIE | (*moving in*) How much respect did *you* show? You — or your mother?

(*Deliberately,* KATHLEEN *turns her back. He steps up close behind her and puts his arms round her.*)

KATH | (*struggling*) Get off me!

RITCHIE | (*not hurrying*) I'm a lot stronger than you are.

(*He forces her round to face him, one hand travelling up under her sweater.*)

KATH | Get your filthy hands off — pig!

(She drags her right arm free and hits him full in the face, startling him and enabling her to break free.)

KATH Keep away from me in future! I wouldn't look twice, not if you were the last man on earth.

RITCHIE *(grabbing her viciously by the wrist)* You'll do as I say, from now on, you and that miserable mother of yours —

KATH *(gasping)* Breaking my arm —

(He pulls forcibly and she cries out as she goes into his hungry embrace.)

RITCHIE Starting *now*.

(He bends his mouth to hers — then draws back, as there is a loud bark outside the door, followed by an anxious scratching and snuffling. A man's voice is heard from the yard outside.)

CLUFF *(off)* Clive! Steady, lad. *(Nearer.)* Steady.

RITCHIE *(releasing her)* It's Cluff.

(He pulls away from her, stares at the door and puts his hands behind his back. There is a characteristic knock before the yard-door swings open, to reveal CALEB CLUFF and his dog on the threshold. CLUFF was once a detective-sergeant, in charge of the two-man C.I.D. in this locality. He has been retired for some time but remains a law unto himself. He carries a thick, chestnut walking-stick and looks not like the policeman he used to be but more like a typical Dales farmer, an impression to which the dog CLIVE, a black-and-white border collie, undoubtedly contributes.)

CLUFF We won't be needing you for a bit — stay.

(He steps inside, shutting the dog out.)

RITCHIE How-do, Mr Cluff. On the old job again, are we?

(CLUFF *ignores him, crossing to* KATHLEEN.)

CLUFF — Are you all right, Kathleen?

KATH — (*flustered*) We weren't expecting you. You should have let us know —

CLUFF — I thought I ought to walk over, see how you were getting on.

RITCHIE — Just another — social call then, is it?

(CLUFF *moves to the table, where he stands looking at the parcels. Away from him,* KATHLEEN *tugs at her sweater and makes herself tidy.* CLUFF *does not appear to notice this — but he misses nothing.*)

CLUFF — Been down to Gunnarshaw?

KATH — I just got back. Shopping.

CLUFF — (*his back to her*) You should have stuck to the road.

KATH — I took the short cut through the fields —

CLUFF — Your feet are soaking. If I were you I'd change my socks — you'll catch your death.

KATH — (*obediently*) Right.

CLUFF — And I'd put this loose change away before you go. (*He looks at* RITCHIE.) In case it walks.

(KATHLEEN *reaches for a cocoa-tin on shelves at the rear, removes the lid and drops the change inside. Then she thrusts the tin on the table, uncapped.*)

KATH — Uncle Caleb —

(*She stops short.*)

CLUFF — I'll still be here when you come down. He won't.

(KATHLEEN *goes out* DR, *leaving the door ajar.* CLUFF *removes his hat and coat.*)

RITCHIE	'Uncle Caleb'! Anybody'd think you two were related —
CLUFF	Calling me that? She knows me well enough.
RITCHIE	I'm not disputing that.
	(CLUFF *is at the table, where a brightly coloured bandanna, knotted by its corners, has caught his attention. He starts to untie it casually.*)
CLUFF	Somebody been picking mushrooms?
RITCHIE	What's wrong with that?
CLUFF	Got 'em before the rain set in, did you? Must have — you're as dry as a bone. (*Turns to him.*) Nothing else to do, to occupy your time?
RITCHIE	What have I done wrong now?
CLUFF	(*obliquely*) Nowt like making hay while the sun shines, is there?
RITCHIE	Come again?
CLUFF	It's no more than a couple of days since your uncle died.
RITCHIE	Nobody's been shedding any tears, that I've seen.
CLUFF	Just his wife and daughter now then? Easy pickings. (*A beat.*) If you've got any sense, you'll leave Kathleen well alone.
RITCHIE	Friends, that's all we are — friends! (*As* CLUFF *regards him.*) Ask her, if you don't believe me.
CLUFF	I don't usually warn people twice over.
RITCHIE	Anyway, they'd have a job on now, wouldn't they? At Daneghyll Farm — without me?
CLUFF	It'd sell.
RITCHIE	Maybe it wouldn't have to.

(CLUFF *darts him a look, but all he gets is the return of the smirk, as* RITCHIE *crosses upstage and unhooks a sack from behind the door, tying it round him to form a rough apron.* CLUFF'S *attention has been drawn towards the hall. The door* DR *is pushed open and* DR HEWITT *enters.*)

HEWITT   Caleb —

CLUFF   'Evening.

(WILLIAM HEWITT — *'Doctor Bill'* — *is the father-figure type of rural practitioner: a small, wiry man with a mop of snow-white hair. He is in his seventies, a person normally of quiet good humour, but at the moment his face is serious. He wears an overcoat and a felt hat which he removes as he comes in. Like* KATHLEEN'S, *his shoes are wet and muddy.*)

HEWITT   Is Nell about?

RITCHIE   I'll tell her we've got a houseful —

(*He starts for the inner door as* HEWITT *unbuttons his coat to flap rain from it.*)

CLUFF   (*blocking* RITCHIE) In my day, the back door used to be good enough for hired help. We left the front for visitors — doctors, and suchlike.

(RITCHIE *changes course for the yard.*)

RITCHIE   We're doing well tonight. Family doctors, superannuated policemen —

HEWITT   (*angrily*) Now look here —

CLUFF   Leave it, doctor: you're wasting your breath.

RITCHIE   (*at door*) Tell you this — this place is more popular with Ted dead than it ever was with him alive!

(*As he exits, the dog barks angrily.*)

(*off*) Get out of it — go on, get off me!

CLUFF	The dog doesn't like being left out o' things and he knows his friends.
HEWITT	He'll get drenched out there —
CLUFF	Not my dog. He's from farming stock: he'll find cover quicker than we could.
HEWITT	(*crosses to fire*) This is the worst September we've had for years. More like the depths of winter.
CLUFF	That'll come soon enough. Think they'll keep that lad on, do you — without Ted?
HEWITT	He's got nowhere else to go.
CLUFF	I wouldn't like him knocking round my house.
HEWITT	Nor me.
CLUFF	How old would he be when they took him in?
HEWITT	Sixteen, thereabouts. Ted was the only remaining relative when the boy was orphaned.
CLUFF	He's chasing after Kathleen now.
	(*He wanders back to the table, where the parcels and the mushrooms seem to fascinate him. He picks out a large one.*)
HEWITT	(*worried*) Nothing serious though, is it? I mean, Kathleen wouldn't dream of —
CLUFF	(*calmly*) Wouldn't she? (*He takes out a pocket-knife, and opens up a long, keen blade.*) She can be wild when she wants to. Like her mother.
HEWITT	Caleb, I know I shouldn't ask, but — have you got some kind of professional interest in all this?
CLUFF	I haven't got a profession any more.

HEWITT   Sorry. I knew that was out of place.

CLUFF   (*busy with mushroom*) Walked over, did you? You didn't get that wet driving.

HEWITT   The exercise is good for me.

CLUFF   Four miles — at your time of life? You must be fast for a job.

HEWITT   It makes the day pass. (*Smiles gently.*) It didn't occur to me when I took a partner that he'd insist on taking so much of the load off my shoulders.

CLUFF   I thought that was the whole idea?

(*He bisects the mushroom.*)

HEWITT   When my wife was still alive, yes.

(CLUFF *smells one half of the fungus.*)

Anything wrong with those things?

CLUFF   Perfect, I'd say. Fresh-picked.

(*He pops it in his mouth and eats it. During what follows, he carefully wipes his knife, puts it away and tidies the mushrooms back in the bandanna, then tying it up again to leave it as it was. HEWITT meanwhile is filling his pipe.*)

HEWITT   We've missed you in the town these last two days. The High Street doesn't seem the same without you standing in your ginnel.

CLUFF   They don't pay me for that nowadays.

HEWITT   But you still do it.

CLUFF   Force of habit.

HEWITT   Your friend on the fruit-stall couldn't think where you'd got to.

CLUFF   Been asking him, have you?

HEWITT   He asked me. (*Offers pouch.*) Smoke?

CLUFF   No, thanks. I only smoke a pipe at home,
                when I've got summat to think about.

                (HEWITT *lights his pipe as* CLUFF *picks up a
                framed photograph of* KATHLEEN *and her mother,*
                NELL.)

                Takes after her mother, doesn't she?

HEWITT   (*softly*) Dear Nell ... Kathleen couldn't have
                had a better.

CLUFF   Nell's father worked for mine, you know,
                over at Cluff's Head. I've known her as long
                as I've known you.

HEWITT   (*wistfully*) A lot of water's gone under the
                bridge since then.

CLUFF   We grew up together, practically. The two of
                us. And your Alan.

HEWITT   That's the first time anyone's mentioned his
                name for years. (*Making himself cheer up.*)
                D'you know, I sometimes think he spent his
                happiest days at Cluff's Head with you and
                your family.

CLUFF   Aye. (*Replaces picture.*)

HEWITT   (*glances at watch*) Is that the time? I must be
                getting on —

CLUFF   A minute ago you'd time to spare.

HEWITT   Tonight's one of the two per week that I'm
                allowed a surgery. (*Buttons coat.*) You'll be
                staying?

CLUFF   Just for a word, yes.

HEWITT   Would you tell Nell everything's in order for
                tomorrow?

CLUFF   The funeral? (*Nods.*) I will.

                (*The dog barks suddenly outside, and we hear*
                NELL's *voice as she calms him down.*)

NELL   (*off*) All right, Clive — good boy! Good boy.

              (HEWITT *walks to the yard door and opens it. She
              is on the doorstep, stroking* CLUFF'S *dog.* NELL
              NORTON *is in her early fifties, a countrywoman
              who carries her years well. She is basically
              attractive, though clad at the moment for heavy
              work about the farm.*)

              (*looks up at him*) Hello, Doctor Bill.

              (*She enters, the dog following her.*)

CLUFF   (*snaps fingers*) Here, Clive. Lie down, lad —
              down.

NELL   Ritchie said you wanted me.

              (RITCHIE *comes in behind her.*)

HEWITT   I just called in to confirm the final details.
              The undertakers will be here at ten in the
              morning, and there's to be a preliminary
              service at the chapel. All quite simple and
              straightforward.

              (NELL *nods, as* RITCHIE *steps in.*)

RITCHIE   And cheap, we hope. It right scared him you
              know, me Uncle Ted. Being put down, I
              mean. Allus told me he wanted to be
              cremated.

CLUFF   Did he, now? That's interesting.

RITCHIE   Ah, well — he confided in me, you see.
              'Course, I was his favourite . . . in many ways.

HEWITT   Tell Kathleen I stopped by. Caleb's here to
              keep you company.

              (*He goes out into the yard.* RITCHIE *looks from
              one to the other.*)

RITCHIE   You two must have a lot to talk about. I'll
              leave you to it.

              (*He follows* HEWITT *out, closing the door.* CLUFF
              has found a length of binder-twine in his pocket

and is attaching it to CLIVE'S *collar as a makeshift lead as* NELL, *without speaking to him, takes off her hat and coat to hang them up. Offstage, a cow bawls mournfully.*)

CLUFF   They don't come like Dr Hewitt any more; they never will again.

NELL   (*quietly*) Alan might have carried on the family tradition.

CLUFF   If he'd lived.

NELL   I don't know what we'd have done without the doctor these last two days.

CLUFF   And I've done nowt.

NELL   It wasn't expected of you.

          (*She crosses to the sink and looks out of the window, where she shivers slightly.*)

CLUFF   What's going on, Nell?

NELL   (*changes the subject*) We'll have frost if the sky clears. (*Pause.*) The summers aren't what they used to be, when we were young —

CLUFF   Nothing ever is.

          (*She turns and looks at him. He moves away — his turn to change the subject.*)

          How's Kathleen taking it?

NELL   Is that what brought you here tonight — Kathleen?

CLUFF   Amongst other things.

NELL   We haven't seen you, either of us, since the day my husband died.

          (*The cow — or another — bawls again.* CLUFF *cocks his head at the noise.*)

CLUFF   Hasn't Ritchie had enough rope here yet?

NELL   Or was it me, Caleb?

CLUFF	It's not your job to bring the beasts in — not with a man about the place.
NELL	Ritchie does all the milking —
CLUFF	Any more than it was your job to be up the moor when I dropped in two days ago to see how Ted was doing.
	(*Pause.*)
NELL	I should have known. So it's not my welfare you're concerned about?
CLUFF	Isn't it, lass?
	(*She continues her steady look, then gives a slight shake of the head as if his drift defeats her, and moves away to untie the larger of the two parcels.*)
NELL	You stayed away a full forty-eight hours, just when we needed you most.
CLUFF	And you never asked yourself why?
NELL	(*unwrapping parcel*) The doctor's been coming to Ted off and on for months now —
CLUFF	What's that got to do with —
NELL	(*a sudden flare*) Don't you trust him? Don't *they*? He's given his life to this town! (*Controllng herself, with effort.*) Do they think he's got so old now he's incapable of telling how his patients die?
CLUFF	There's no need for all this, Nell.
NELL	You should have gone on keeping away. If they know you've been here, that lot in Gunnarshaw will be certain I helped him into his grave.
	(*She takes a new, black mourning-dress from the parcel and drapes it over the back of a chair. KATHLEEN enters DR, wearing slippers, her stockings changed.*)
KATH	I put the change in the tin.

NELL   Right.

                (*She replaces the lid on the cocoa-tin, putting it
                back on the shelves. There is a silence as*
                KATHLEEN *goes to the sink to exchange her
                slippers for a pair of wellingtons. Outside, the cow
                bawls again — and is now joined by others.*)

CLUFF   (*testily*) Isn't he *ever* going to get round to it?

KATH   Who?

CLUFF   That Ritchie — you said the milking was his
                job —

KATH   Everybody lets us down, in time.

NELL   Get the hens seen to.

KATH   I'm just going.

                (CLUFF *drops* CLIVE's *lead and fetches her a
                basket from the table.*)

CLUFF   Ritchie's out there. Take the dog.

KATH   Thanks. Come on, Clive.

                (*The collie goes out with her, happily.*)

NELL   She wanted you.

CLUFF   I know.

NELL   Compared to you, her dad meant nothing to
                her —

CLUFF   Don't say that.

NELL   Why shouldn't I? They hated the sight of
                each other. (*Thoughtfully.*) At least, if
                Kathleen wasn't in the house when Ted died
                — they know where she'd gone. A lot of
                them saw her shopping, down in
                Gunnarshaw. (*Making too much of it.*) She goes
                down there every day —

CLUFF   I know.

NELL   ·   (*presses*) We have to eat, and there are no shops nearer —

CLUFF   Leave it be, Nell.

NELL   How can I? When you called round that day you found a dying man all alone in an empty house. What were you supposed to think?

CLUFF   I didn't think anything, except to get a doctor —

NELL   I'd gone up to get the sheep for dipping. Ritchie had a drain to dig in the top pasture —

CLUFF   I know where Ritchie was. I saw him on my way back —

NELL   But you didn't see me. Nobody did. And that's what they're on about now — isn't it?

CLUFF   (*evading this*) If he'd downed tools when I told him to — if he'd come back here and seen to Ted he'd have arrived before Dr Hewitt.

NELL   Ritchie didn't care whether Ted lived or died. (*Slight pause.*) Who did, Caleb? Who did? (*She leaves him, going to the second parcel and tearing its wrapping roughly away. She thrusts a pair of shoes on to the table.*)

CLUFF   Nay, not new shoes on a table.

NELL   They're not new, they've been to the cobbler's. Anyway, what difference would it make, to luck like mine?

(*Nevertheless, she places them elsewhere.*)

CLUFF   Kathleen needn't have gone in today. I could have picked that stuff up for you.

NELL   We didn't know you'd be coming.

CLUFF   Or Sergeant Barker could have collected 'em. He's out this way most evenings, courting Annie Croft's daughter.

NELL	That's another one who's given us a miss — Annie Croft.
CLUFF	She'll be round.
NELL	Anybody else dead, she'd have been on the doorstep before you could say 'knife'.
CLUFF	Aye, she collects drama, does Annie. But what with a grown-up family to manage, then coming in to cook and clean for me — she's got her hands full.
NELL	Why do you keep changing the subject? I know what they all think I did — the next thing is to find a reason. And they won't have far to look, now you've been here.
CLUFF	Calm down lass, will you?
NELL	(*erect*) But you can tell them this when they start on at you. They're right in one thing —I'm *glad* he's dead!
CLUFF	(*gently*) They've already started.
	(*Offstage, the sound of a souped-up sports car is heard, driving up to the farm.*)
	Talk of the devil . . .
	(*The car stops outside.*)
NELL	Who is it?
CLUFF	Barker.
NELL	(*biting her lip*) How do you know?
CLUFF	Because there's no other car in Yorkshire that can make a row like that.
NELL	You weren't content then to come here by yourself?
CLUFF	Just won't let it alone, will you? Why is that?
	(*A knock comes at the front door, off* R. *Neither of them moves. The knock is repeated.*)

CLUFF	Aren't you going to answer it?
NELL	Why should I? People walk in and out of here as if the place belongs to them.
ANNIE	(*off*) Nell! Nell, are you in?
CLUFF	It's Annie.

(*A friendly tap on the door* DR. NELL *turns, as* ANNIE CROFT *comes in. She is* CLUFF'S '*daily*' — *a round, apple-cheeked woman, whose forthrightness is a screen for her underlying compassion. She pauses to take* CLUFF *in, and registers her usual disapproval of him.*)

ANNIE	So you're here, then?
CLUFF	Looks like it. (*He turns away and sits down.*)
ANNIE	They said you would be. (*To* NELL.) Now I've landed, is there anything I can do?
NELL	We'll manage, Annie. We've been managing —
ANNIE	It's such a long pull, on foot. But when they called at the cottage looking for him, and offered me a lift —
NELL	Police business, was it?
ANNIE	(*carefully*) They didn't say, love.
NELL	But they knew where to find him. Why don't you bring them in?
CLUFF	(*as* ANNIE *glances at him*) Go on — have the courage of your own iniquity.
ANNIE	(*scowls*) I'm not talking to you.
CLUFF	You were looking at me.

(ANNIE *goes and calls through the open door.*)

ANNIE	David! (*To* NELL.) It's only Barker.
CLUFF	Are you sure?

(DETECTIVE SERGEANT DAVID BARKER *enters*
DR, *a young, fresh-faced, prematurely balding,*
plain-clothes policeman. At the moment he is
feeling somewhat out of his depth.)

BARKER   (*stiffly*) Good evening, Mrs Norton. (*As* NELL
              nods.) I'd, er, I'd like to express my deepest
              sympathy —

NELL   Thank you.

              (*She turns to pick up the shoes and the dress. Lost*
              for words, BARKER *looks at* CLUFF. *He is met with*
              a frosty glare.)

BARKER   Perhaps I'd better wait outside ...

CLUFF   You'll stop here, *Sergeant* Barker.

ANNIE   (*sternly*) Both of you — remember where you
              are, and keep your voices down.

NELL   Now you've come all this way, Annie, you'd
              like to see him?

ANNIE   I'd better pay me last respects. Ted made a
              lot of mistakes, but he was a good lad at
              heart.

NELL   He's upstairs.

              (*She goes out into the hall.* ANNIE *follows, pausing*
              at the door.)

ANNIE   Have you gone out of your senses, Caleb
              Cluff? As if there aren't enough tongues
              wagging already!

              (*She follows* NELL *out, leaving the door open.*
              BARKER *moves over to close it.*)

CLUFF   Right. Let's have it.

              (BARKER *shuffles his feet.*)

              'When they called', Annie said. There's only
              one of you — so where's the other?

BARKER   (*uncomfortably*) Caleb —

CLUFF   Whose idea was it to follow me here? Yours
            — Annie's — or Inspector Mole's?

BARKER   We're all in agreement at the station —

CLUFF   Are you? Things must have changed a bit
             since my day.

BARKER   What I mean is, it can't be left like this, can
             it? (*Pause.*) Ted Norton's death, I mean.

CLUFF   Can't it?

BARKER   We've been waiting all day, hoping you'd call
             in.

CLUFF   Consultant now, am I? Nobody's mentioned
             any fees.

BARKER   We waited all day yesterday as well.

CLUFF   Just in case you've forgotten, I don't work
             there anymore.

BARKER   I think you know what I'm getting at,
             sergeant.

CLUFF   Don't call me that.

BARKER   Sorry, it just slipped out.

CLUFF   Don't let it slip out again.

BARKER   There's been a lot of talk about Mrs Norton.
             (*Then, hastily.*) We're sure there's not a word
             of truth in it. All the inspector's trying to do
             is stop the gossip, all these rumours flying
             about —

CLUFF   He's after more than that, if he'd risk riding
             in your car.

BARKER   The way he put it was — you being an old
             friend of the family, you might be a bit, well,
             offended if we —

CLUFF   Did anything official, behind my back?

BARKER   (*patiently, from long experience of him*) We just
             don't want to tread on anybody's toes.

CLUFF	Mine haven't felt any pain, as yet.
BARKER	Inspector Mole respects your feelings —
CLUFF	Does he? When did he start doing that?
BARKER	(*coming to the point*) He's waiting in the car. Will you go out and have a word with him?
CLUFF	No.
BARKER	Why not?
CLUFF	He likes a good think, does Mole. If he sits there long enough, and thinks hard enough he might just get round to the truth.

(RITCHIE *returns from the yard, the sack about his shoulders damp and stinking.*)

And what have you been up to?

RITCHIE	Only doing what I'm paid to do — occasionally.
CLUFF	(*rises*) All I can say is, somebody's pouring money down the drain! (*He strides out* ULC, *slamming the door.*)
RITCHIE	You never know where you are, with that chap!
BARKER	You're telling me.

(RITCHIE *gets himself a basin out of the wall cupboard and sets about transferring the mushrooms into it.*)

RITCHIE	Can't stop hisself bobbying. But Ted allus used to say Cluff got off on the wrong foot when he came out the Army. Police force was second choice it seems, when his brother got Cluff's Head Farm. (*The usual smirk.*) I know all the family history, y'see.
BARKER	(*moving in*) Mushrooms?

RITCHIE   (*nodding*) First taste I've had this year. What there was, you see, they gave to the invalid. He allus fancied mushrooms.

BARKER   I wouldn't mind a few myself — take back to the digs —

RITCHIE   You'll have to go and find some then, 'cos these are booked.

                 (*He rolls the bandanna up and stuffs it in his pocket, as he glances through the open door to the hall.*)

                 Hello, Here's another of 'em. Place is running wick wi' coppers tonight!

                 (INSPECTOR PERCY MOLE *sticks his head round the door* DR. *He wears an immaculate uniform which includes at present his greatcoat and cap.* MOLE *sports a toothbrush moustache, and favours as a symbol of the authority of which he is somewhat uncertain, a highly polished swagger-stick.*)

MOLE   (*officiously*) What's happening, Barker?

BARKER   Nothing, sir.

MOLE   I might have known!

RITCHIE   All this poking and prying about — it'd make a feller right nervous, if Cluff hadn't as good as been here when Ted snuffed it.

MOLE   (*advances*) Don't I know your face?

RITCHIE   You should.

MOLE   What's your name?

RITCHIE   Everybody calls me Ritchie; but on Sundays, it's Richard Norton.

MOLE   Unless I'm very much mistaken, you and I have met before — officially.

RITCHIE   Aw, what's one 'drunk and disorderly' between friends?

MOLE   You'll find out if we have you up again.
            (*Turns on his subordinate.*) Now then, Barker
            — where is Cluff?

BARKER   Gone out, sir.

MOLE   A long-standing habit, when I'm in the
            vicinity.

RITCHIE   One thing about the Cluffs: they all end up
            where they began, back on the land.

MOLE   Speak when you're spoken to! (*Turns sharply
            to* BARKER, *then just as sharply turns back again.*)
            What do you mean?

RITCHIE   (*significantly*) It doesn't grow in bottles . . .

MOLE   What doesn't?

RITCHIE   Milk. That white stuff you put in tea.

            (*He turns away, to put the basin of mushrooms on
            the shelves. There is a beat, as the penny
            drops . . .*)

MOLE   You don't mean to tell me Cluff's gone
            milking cows? It can't be true, Barker!

BARKER   They are short-handed, sir.

RITCHIE   He's probably just getting the hang of things,
            in case he wants —

BARKER   (*shortly*) Watch it, you.

            (RITCHIE *collects a bucket from under the sink,
            taking it to the boiler to ladle water into it.* MOLE
            and BARKER *exchange glances, and* MOLE *purses
            his lips.*)

RITCHIE   Tell you this: he'd rather be running
            Daneghyll Farm, I'll bet, than wearing his
            boot-leather out traipsing up and down the
            fells wi' time on his hands. (*He takes the bucket
            out,* ULC.)

MOLE   Now that we're alone, Barker — what do you
            honestly make of all this?

BARKER   Not a lot, sir. Mainly talk, if you ask me. I thought we agreed in the car —

MOLE   We agreed a great deal in the car, because Mrs Croft's ears were flapping ten to the dozen. But all these slurs and insinuations — there's no smoke without fire.

BARKER   You shouldn't listen to Ritchie —

MOLE   It's not only that layabout, it's everyone in Gunnarshaw! (*Taps stick against leg, looking round room.*) And he's right about one thing — Cluff was always more of a farmer than a policeman.

BARKER   I still say there couldn't possibly be anything between him and Mrs Norton after all these years.

MOLE   (*always suspicious*) Let's hope that's true.

BARKER   The more they talk about Caleb, the more he'll give 'em something to talk about.

MOLE   'Caleb' — it's an extraordinary name! I've often wondered ... (*He glances at* BARKER, *but finds him busy consulting his notebook.*) Oh never mind, it's not important. But thank the Lord I was born in a respectable city, not out here in this — this Biblical back o' beyond!

           (BARKER, *absorbed, makes no reply, so* MOLE *tours the room, pausing to set the rocking-chair in motion. Its hinges squeal mournfully.*)

           Antediluvian! I've seen rooms like this in folk-museums. Do they know what century they're living in?

BARKER   Besides, the arrangements have all been finalised.

MOLE   Arrangements?

BARKER   For the funeral, sir.

MOLE   Really Barker, you're quite imponderable at
              times. You picked that up from Cluff, I
              suppose?

BARKER   (*looks up*) All I said was the funeral's been
              fixed, sir.

MOLE   When did you check up on that?

BARKER   When did you?

              (MOLE *does not answer. Instead, he halts the
              chair, places it meticulously in position, then looks
              round the room.*)

MOLE   Mind you, this primitive atmosphere would
              suit Cluff down to the ground. At his
              farewell dinner, they said he should be listed
              as an Ancient Monument. Rather
              appropriate, I thought!

BARKER   Very droll. (*He has strolled near the shelves and
              is studying the mushrooms.*) Now, the
              undertaker couldn't move until the registrar
              had been informed. Therefore there must
              have been a death certificate. (*Takes basin
              down.*)

MOLE   And the patient was attended by Dr Hewitt,
              another relic of the past. They're all tarred
              with the same — what have you got there?

BARKER   (*hands basin over, innocently*) Mushrooms, sir.

MOLE   Do stop thinking about your stomach,
              Barker. (*Examines one.*) You can't eat them
              raw, anyway. Thanks to your former
              superior, I've had no tea, either. (*Drops it back
              in place.*)

              (NELL *enters* DR, *followed by* ANNIE CROFT. *She
              crosses straight to* MOLE *and takes the basin from
              him.*)

NELL   Excuse me.

MOLE   I wasn't being inquisitive —

ANNIE	(*shortly*) That's summat fresh.
NELL	You came to see me, inspector?
MOLE	Since I — er — happened to be in the neighbourhood, I thought it only right and proper to call and offer my condolences —
NELL	I see. Kind of you. (*She sets the basin down on the table*.)
MOLE	Also, we are in search of your friend Mr Cluff, and I was given to understand —
NELL	(*to* BARKER) Caleb hasn't gone, has he?
BARKER	I believe he's helping Ritchie.
NELL	I'll get him for you. (*She goes out* ULC.)
MOLE	She called him by his first name, did you catch on?
ANNIE	(*promptly*) Everybody does! Except me — and I've got other names for him. Inspector Mole, you gave me your solemn promise that you'd stop in the car till we got him out —
MOLE	That is so. But my patience, like my time, is strictly limited. (*As she tries to speak.*) When we called at the cottage you seemed just as concerned as we were.
ANNIE	What about?
MOLE	If we should find Cluff here . . .
ANNIE	(*glowers*) If *you* should find him, you mean!
BARKER	They're old friends. It's understandable, surely?
ANNIE	That's why he called in that day to see how Ted was. And it's nowt to do with him if Ted died all on his own.
MOLE	You mean before the doctor got here?
ANNIE	Haven't they told you that?

MOLE   Who tells me anything? All I heard was, when Cluff arrived that afternoon he found a very sick man and immediately summoned a doctor. You say he left the patient all alone in this God-forsaken hole?

ANNIE   (*as to a child*) He had to go back to his cottage to use the phone.

MOLE   Twenty minutes' walk? You're joking.

ANNIE   What else could he do, with nobody on hand —

MOLE   Do my eyes deceive me?

ANNIE   Pardon?

MOLE   (*points*) Is that a telephone, or isn't it?

BARKER   Yes sir, but it's been out of order.

ANNIE   The milk cheque's about the only ready cash Ted had left, and it doesn't come in that often. What did he have to pay telephone bills with?

MOLE   (*starts towards it*) Been cut off, had she?

ANNIE   (*blocks his path*) Hasn't he taught you nowt?

MOLE   I'm sorry?

ANNIE   Can't you see what's going through his mind? They've never had it easy, up here on the fell. You try these moors in winter — scratting and scraping a living! Summer's not much better —

MOLE   Then why, for heaven's sake, didn't he marry her all those years ago and save her from it?

ANNIE   He would have, if he'd had his way! But she was a lot younger then and didn't know her own mind. Chucked him over, didn't she, for somebody else — somebody not fit to lick his boots. Aw, you don't know the half of it.

MOLE   I'm learning.

ANNIE   How do you suppose he's feeling now — now she's been left, with nothing? (*She turns away.* MOLE *goes to the phone, picks it up, listens and then dials.*)

MOLE   Operator?

ANNIE   (*disturbed*) David, can't you stop him? It's all wrong, barging in on a bereavement —

MOLE   (*into phone*) Police, here — nothing, thank you. Just checking. (*Hangs up.*) Cut off, indeed!

(KATHLEEN *comes in from the yard with her basket now filled with eggs. The sight of* MOLE *stops her in her tracks.*)

ANNIE   It's all right, love; they're only after Cluff. Give me that. (*Takes basket to table.*) Follow him about like sheep, they do. Still . . .

KATH   (*confronts* MOLE) What do you want from us? Isn't my mother ever to have any peace?

MOLE   Control yourself, young lady —

KATH   About my father, is it? What about him? He couldn't help dying, could he? Nobody can! What's Ritchie been telling you all? (*When nobody answers.*) He's been on about Uncle Caleb. (*To* MOLE.) That's right, isn't it?

MOLE   (*eyes widening*) Uncle?

KATH   We've never had anybody but him — now everybody's trying to turn him against us!

ANNIE   Kathleen!

KATH   (*an outburst*) You, as well! You hate him mixing with us — because we're the Nortons, aren't we? We're bad news! Cluff's the only friend we've got! (*She stops short, choking back a sob, and hurries out into the hall.*)

ANNIE   (*blaming* MOLE) Satisfied? (*Shaking her head, she goes out after the girl.*)

MOLE   (*turning to* BARKER) I never said a blind word!

BARKER   The girl's upset, sir, naturally.

MOLE   Naturally! Whereas the mother seems as cool
             as a cucumber —

BARKER   I keep saying, it's all talk about Mrs Norton —

MOLE   Is it indeed? I'm sorry, Barker, I intend to
             get to the bottom of this. If bottom it has.

BARKER   Aren't you forgetting, sir? Criminal
             investigation's my department now, in
             Gunnarshaw.

MOLE   (*severely*) Quite. But unfortunately you seem
             to have fallen victim to some kind of mental
             inertia. If you won't move on this, I'll find
             somebody who will!

BARKER   You wouldn't be thinking of going to the
             coroner — over my head?

MOLE   I shall do whatever I deem necessary.

BARKER   It's not a sudden death we're dealing with —

MOLE   No. But we are dealing with a death in
             suspicious circumstances.

BARKER   *Questionable* circumstances. That's as far as I'll
             go.

             (*This has a ring of* CLUFF *about it that makes*
             MOLE *cock a beady eye at him.*)

MOLE   I sometimes think you worked under Cluff so
             long, you can't see the wood for the trees!

BARKER   (*admits*) I learned a lot from him. Amongst
             other things — in C.I.D. — to proceed with
             caution.

MOLE   You make him sound like a traffic-warden.

BARKER   (*doggedly*) Especially in a domestic incident.

MOLE   Be that as it may, ex-Sergeant Cluff is no
             longer on the strength.

BARKER   So?

MOLE   (*drawing himself up*) As I see it, justice must
             not only be done, it must be seen to be done.
             And I am here to see to the seeing of it.

CLUFF   (*his voice from the doorway*) Aren't we lucky?
             (*He is standing there, in shirt-sleeves.*)

MOLE   Ah! At long last, the mountain has come to
             Mahomet.

CLUFF   Who sent for me, and why?

MOLE   (*not immediately*) Barker?

BARKER   (*stolid*) I didn't say a word, sir.

CLUFF   Well? I'm waiting — and there's work to be
             done.

MOLE   None of your tantrums, if you don't mind. If
             you've stopped thinking of yourself, at least
             consider the dignity of the Force you once,
             er ... embellished.

CLUFF   (*coming in*) The Police Service won't suffer
             from anything I do.

MOLE   Now you've set us quite straight about that,
             may we proceed?

             (CLUFF *halts at the table, looking down at the
             basket of eggs.*)

CLUFF   I see Kathleen's been through?

BARKER   She's upstairs, with Mrs Croft.

CLUFF   If you've done owt to upset that lass —

MOLE   She upset herself. Just at the moment, I'm
             more interested in her mother. I take it she is
             within call?

CLUFF   If wanted. (*As* MOLE *snorts.*) Do you want her
             — and if so, why?

MOLE   There are certain aspects of recent events
              here that I find somewhat disturbing.

CLUFF   Let's have it in plain English. Did Ted
              Norton die, or was he pushed?

MOLE   (*turning to* BARKER) And you were concerned
              about his finer feelings!

CLUFF   What's the official answer?

MOLE   There isn't one — till we're in full possession
              of the facts. That's why we're here.

CLUFF   Next question: who did it, his own next of
              kin?

MOLE   (*stiffly*) At the moment, all opinions are
              reserved.

CLUFF   (*shortly*) Mine isn't.

BARKER   (*to* CLUFF) Ritchie happens to live here, as
              well, you know.

CLUFF   A choice of three, then. Or is it four?

MOLE   Four?

CLUFF   Have a little think, inspector.

              (*He starts to roll down his shirt-sleeves.*)

MOLE   Turning your back on matters isn't going to
              help.

CLUFF   I'm not. You carry on. Got any theories?

MOLE   (*swallows*) Everything seems to hinge on that
              vital half-hour between you leaving the house
              and Dr Hewitt arriving.

BARKER   But what if it started before that?

MOLE   Don't interrupt when I'm in full flow —

BARKER   Look — we're all assuming Norton's last
              illness was the same as the previous ones. He
              suffered from his inside, Annie told us that
              in the car. Suppose somebody knew about
              that: suppose they took advantage of it?

MOLE   (*interested*) The stomach. Poison, do you
            mean?

BARKER   (*nods*) That would account for the death
            certificate. If the symptoms were similar.

CLUFF   So the doctor's in on this, as well?

BARKER   No, no. He could have been going on the
            previous medical history. I was thinking more
            of Ritchie.

MOLE   Rubbish. He'd never have the nerve. (*On a
            thought.*) I'll grant you this, though — poison
            is a *woman's* weapon.

CLUFF   (*to* BARKER) Been lending him library books
            again, have you? You'll regret it.

BARKER   There's one sure way ... (*He breaks off,
            looking at* CLUFF.)

CLUFF   Go on, Barker — follow it through.

BARKER   I was going to say ... legally, there's one
            sure way of finding out.

            (*The dog barks excitedly, off, and* NELL *enters
            from the yard, carrying* CLUFF'S *old tweed jacket.*)

NELL   You left this in the barn. (*She hands it to him,
            as the dog runs in through the open door.*) Clive,
            too.

            (BARKER *calls the dog as* CLUFF *starts to put on
            his jacket.*)

BARKER   Here! Here, boy! (*He makes a fuss of* CLIVE.)

NELL   Well, inspector — will there be anything
            further?

MOLE   There may be. Indeed there may be. Cluff,
            would you care to explain the situation?

CLUFF   Me? Not likely.

MOLE   But —

CLUFF   Don't forget, I'm just an interested bystander.

(ANNIE *returns*, DR.)

ANNIE	I knew you'd come in, I heard the dog. (*As* NELL *tries to speak.*) Before I go — you'll need a meal ready when you get back in the morning. You can leave that to me.
NELL	There's no need —
CLUFF	How's Kathleen?
ANNIE	(*more subdued*) She's quietened down.
NELL	Why do you ask?
ANNIE	It's nothing, love. She got herself a bit worked up.
NELL	What's been said?
BARKER	Nothing at all.
ANNIE	There's too much nosey-parkering going on, that's the trouble. They ought to go their various ways, and leave you both in peace!
NELL	If you need me, I'll be with my daughter. (*She goes out* DR.)
ANNIE	What she means is, they'd rather have your space than your company.
MOLE	Thank you, Mrs Croft, you've said enough.
ANNIE	I haven't started yet! (*She jams her hat on firmly.*) I'll be sat sitting in the car. (*She marches out* DR.)
CLUFF	(*dolefully*) That's torn it! She'll give me a terrible breakfast in the morning. (*He slumps into a chair.*)
BARKER	Caleb, a post mortem would settle all this, once and for all.
MOLE	Won't you at least speak to Mrs Norton? It's far better if she volunteers permission.
CLUFF	And let her know you think she might have killed him?

MOLE   (*arguing the point*) If she's as innocent as you
                believe, there's no valid reason for refusing —

CLUFF   Black's black, isn't it? And white's white?
                There's nothing in between. That's all police
                work's taught you?

MOLE   (*exploding*) Goddammit, man! Can't you see
                I'm trying to *help* you both?

BARKER   Inspector —

CLUFF   Don't bother, Barker. You're wasting your
                time, both of you.

MOLE   (*delivering his ultimatum*) The matter has to be
                resolved, one way or the other. Barker
                doesn't know which leg to stand on. Either
                you move, Cluff, or I do. That is final.

                (MOLE *stalks out* DR. CLUFF *sighs, tired, and
                stares into the fire.* BARKER *watches him,
                undecided.*)

CLUFF   Go on Barker, scoot. You don't work for me
                any more.

BARKER   That's not fair, sergeant ... (*He breaks off, as
                *CLUFF *looks at him.*)

CLUFF   (*bleakly*) And don't ever call me that again.
                Least of all, under this roof.

BARKER   (*colours up*) Some sort of crime, is it?

CLUFF   There's reasons, lad if you dig deep enough.

                (BARKER *exits* DR *without another word.* CLUFF
                *rises to get his raincoat. He is pulling it on as
                *RITCHIE *appears from the yard. He comes in and
                clatters his bucket under the sink, then doffs his
                sack and hangs it up behind the door. Outside, the
                sports car explodes into action and drives away.*)

RITCHIE   They're off, then?

(He gets no reply from CLUFF, *who is reaching for his hat.* RITCHIE'S *smirk widens, as he helps himself to water in the lading-can from the boiler and takes it to the sink to have a peremptory wash.)*

RITCHIE   Old Ted seems to be more bother dead than he ever was alive. I think I'll miss him, mind you.

CLUFF   Don't come it: you two have been at daggers drawn ever since I've known you.

RITCHIE   It was different at the finish. Best of friends, we were. Uncle Ted was quite — forthcoming. *(He dries himself on the roller-towel briskly, and sits to remove his boots.)*

CLUFF   Going out?

RITCHIE   Both got summat to celebrate, haven't we? That's what I'm doing, anyroad — celebrating! And I'm leaving you and Auntie Nell to celebrate all on your own.

CLUFF   Taking Kathleen with you?

RITCHIE   Not tonight. She isn't in the mood.

CLUFF   She never will be, far as you're concerned.

RITCHIE   *(throws boots under sink)* The way you watch over her — it's funny-peculiar, somehow. Summat of her mother in her, is there — summat that brings back old memories? What's the matter, Uncle Caleb — *jealous*?

*(*CLUFF'S *right hand shoots out and grabs him by the shirt-neck, yanking him close.)*

CLUFF   I've just about had enough from you tonight. You start saying things like that and I'll start thinking about breaking your bloody neck. Think on!

(He thrusts RITCHIE *away from him, and the farmhand half-falls against the table.)*

RITCHIE	Keep your sodding hands to yourself, Caleb Cluff. You're not master here yet, and never will be if I can help it! You've lorded it over everybody a bit too much! (*He scrambles up, backing for the hall.*) They've stood it this long down in Gunnarshaw, but you'll get your come-uppance, wait and see!

(*The dog growls, menacingly.*)

CLUFF	No, Clive —
RITCHIE	And it could come anytime now!
CLUFF	Out. (*He takes a step forward, and* RITCHIE *scuttles off,* DR. CLUFF *stands for a moment, pent up. Then all the strength seems to drain out of him and he sags, looking old and tired.*) All right, lad — we'll be off.

(*He collects his stick and then pauses, staring down again at the mushrooms.* NELL *comes in quietly* DR. *She halts at the sight of him, hovering there alone.*)

(*speaking without moving*) You must have passed him on the stairs.

NELL	Ritchie?
CLUFF	If you're too frightened to throw him out, I'll do it for you.

(*There is no answer. He turns to her.*)

NELL	He can't hurt me, Caleb — believe me.
CLUFF	Not even through Kathleen?
NELL	(*crossing to the fire*) I can handle both our lives. I've had to, for a long time now.
CLUFF	Can you think of the pair of 'em — together?
NELL	It won't come to that. I won't let it. Ever.
CLUFF	(*nods slowly*) I had to be sure. (*He walks upstage, putting on his hat.*)

NELL	(*perfectly controlled*) And the funeral?
CLUFF	(*halts, turning*) What about it?
NELL	I just wondered if there's still going to *be* a funeral?
	(KATHLEEN *enters* DR, *pale and drawn.* CLUFF *looks at both of them, searchingly.*)
CLUFF	Come on, Clive. (*He trudges out with the dog.*)
	(*After a moment,* NELL'S *control leaves her, and she sinks into a chair by the hearth, lowering her head in her hands.* KATHLEEN *goes to comfort her.*)
KATH	Try not to worry.
NELL	He won't help us.
KATH	But he'll never turn against us.
NELL	We can't be sure. People always said about Cluff — you'll never separate the man from the policeman.
KATH	They didn't know him like we do. (*A sudden outburst.*) God knows, what we did — it's nothing to be ashamed of!
	(RITCHIE *comes back,* DR. *He has not changed his jeans, but now wears a pair of gaudy trainers and a black leather bomber-jacket, complete with studs and chains. His hair is in a greasy pigtail and his personal stereo is slung round his neck. He seems jubilant.*)
RITCHIE	(*mocking*) Just look at that — every picture tells a story!
	(KATHLEEN *rises and moves away from* NELL. *He goes and takes the cocoa-tin from the shelves, rattles it, then removes the lid and tips its contents into his palm.*)
KATH	What do you think you're doing?

RITCHIE	Helping meself. What with mourning-dresses and trimmings it's a wonder there's owt left in the kitty.
KATH	Put that back!
RITCHIE	Get lost. I've earned it, haven't I?
	(*He pockets the cash, putting the tin on the table.* NELL *rises to her feet.*)
NELL	Earned it — how?
RITCHIE	Keeping me trap shut.
KATH	Mother, he can't —
NELL	Hush.
RITCHIE	(*grinning*) That's why you won't begrudge me some loose change in me pocket. Got to stand me corner you know, down at the Cock and Bottle. (*He preens himself at the mirror.*) All here, weren't they? Inspector Mole — Sergeant Barker — even God-almighty Cluff hisself. (*Slowly.*) And I never said a dicky-bird.
	(KATHLEEN *turns quickly to* NELL.)
NELL	Just let him go.
KATH	But why should we allow him to —
NELL	Quiet!
RITCHIE	(*comes closer*) Various reasons, Little Miss High-and-Mighty. Like what your mother is, and what she's done. If I'd wanted to, lass, I could have put you both in the cart tonight.
KATH	What do you think you know?
RITCHIE	Plenty. (*Savouring it.*) For one thing — I know whose daughter you really are. But I couldn't let on, could I? 'Cos we all love each other, don't we? And there's some things that need keeping in the family. Know what I mean, lovey? (*He puts a warning finger to his lips, winks knowingly, and wanders out.*)

                    (KATHLEEN *turns to her mother but* NELL *ignores
                    her as she watches* RITCHIE *go.*)

KATH   He's lying —

NELL   Go to bed.

KATH   He's got to be lying!

NELL   (*turning*) Didn't you hear me? I said go to
            bed!

KATH   But —

                    (NELL *closes her eyes and holds her head.*)

NELL   (*in desperation*) All I want — for God's sake —
            is to be left alone!

                    (KATHLEEN *shakes her head, slowly and
                    disbelieving, before turning and off* DR. *After a
                    long moment,* NELL'S *arms drop to her sides.
                    Motionless, she gazes again at the open door and
                    down the yard outside. Distantly, the bark of a dog
                    is heard.* CLUFF'S *dog.*)

                    (*Medium fade — to blackout.*)

Scene Two

*Early the next morning. The blind is up and watery sunshine filters
into the kitchen. The basket of eggs has gone from the table, but the
mushrooms remain on the shelves. Simple breakfast things have
been added to the crockery, etc., left on the table from the previous
evening. The bucket from under the sink is missing. The
grandfather clock shows nine a.m.*

KATHLEEN *is huddled in one of the fireside chairs, dressed in a
thick dressing-gown and slippers. Her eyes are red from lack of
sleep and her face is pale and tear-stained.*

*Occasionally, offstage, there are farm noises: hens cluck, a pail
clanks on a stone floor and a sheep bleats.*

NELL *enters from the yard, in working gear and carrying the bucket. She stares at her daughter before dumping it under the sink. She comes towards the table, scans it, then pours milk into a cup.*

NELL Kathleen you haven't touched your breakfast.

    (*Her daughter seems oblivious.*)

    They'll be here with the hearse in less than an hour. Drink some milk at least —

    (*Still silence.* NELL *takes the cup to the draining-board and leaves it there as she removes her coat and hangs it behind the door. She wears no hat.*)

KATH If it's still coming.

NELL (*looks round sharply*) Why do you say that?

KATH Settles it for them, doesn't it ... when Ritchie isn't at the funeral?

NELL (*whispering to herself*) Oh, my God! (*She comes to the girl and draws her to her feet.*) Swear to me — if you've any love left — you stayed in your room all night?

KATH You locked me in — because of him. You didn't come up again till you unlocked the door this morning. And I never went to sleep.

    (NELL *gives her a searching look before she releases her.*)

NELL We must start getting ready.

KATH You first.

    (NELL, *troubled, makes her way to the door* DR. KATHLEEN *stands fixed.*)

KATH And you still won't tell me?

NELL (*halts*) Try not to blame me too much —

KATH   It's him I blame — my father ... *my real*
              father. Tell me his name! You can't hide it
              any more. I know. Ritchie knew.

NELL   (*suddenly*) There's somebody outside —

KATH   (*strangely relieved*) It must be him.

NELL   It can't be! (*As* KATHLEEN's *head jerks round*.) I
              mean, that's too quiet — for Ritchie.

              (*The latch of the yard door is tried carefully from
              the outside, then it swings open to reveal* DR
              HEWITT, *soberly dressed, a black homburg in his
              hand. He comes in*.)

HEWITT   Sorry if I startled you. Too early, I'm afraid —

NELL   Sit down, doctor. There's tea in the pot.

HEWITT   You're not ready. I'll wait in the lane —

NELL   No need. We're just going up to change. Stay
              by the fire, where it's warm.

HEWITT   Thank you. (*He goes to it*.) Well, it'll soon be
              over.

              (KATHLEEN *takes a sharp breath and* NELL *moves
              near to comfort her*.)

NELL   You mustn't give way now —

KATH   Don't touch me!

HEWITT   Kathleen —

              (KATHLEEN *thrusts away from them both, up to the
              open door*.)

KATH   I can't breathe in here! (*She looks outside, then
              turns*.) He's coming down the yard —

NELL   Ritchie?

KATH   Cluff. (*Breaking away*.) It's no good, I can't
              look him in the face! (*She runs off* DR,
              distraught.)

HEWITT   (*takes a step in*) What's gone wrong?

NELL   Trust me. And don't say anything to Caleb.

                (CLUFF *clumps past the window and appears in
                the open doorway. He wears a black tie. There is
                no dog with him. He looks at them, then round the
                room.*)

CLUFF   You shouldn't leave Kathleen by herself on a
                day like this.

NELL   She won't talk to anyone till it's over.

                (CLUFF *glances at* DR HEWITT.)

HEWITT   Too distressed. She's never met death before.

NELL   (*subdued*) I must get ready.

                (*She goes out* DR, *unbuttoning her cardigan.*
                HEWITT *watches her go in some concern.*)

CLUFF   Not the only one, is she?

HEWITT   What?

CLUFF   Distressed.

HEWITT   I think there's more — relief for Nell, than
                anything else. She didn't have much joy out
                of her marriage.

CLUFF   The girl, neither.

HEWITT   And of course they'll both be suffering from
                a sense of guilt.

CLUFF   Guilt?

HEWITT   Because neither of them was here when Ted
                died. But they had the farm to run. (*Strangely
                insistent.*) They couldn't watch over him every
                minute of every day! Perhaps if I'd got here
                sooner I might have saved him but it
                wouldn't have been for long.

CLUFF   He looked bad when I saw him: that's why I
                sent Ritchie back. Or tried to.

HEWITT	Ted's been a dying man for a long time.
CLUFF	Did his wife know that?
HEWITT	I never put it into words. But there are some things you don't need to tell a woman.
CLUFF	(*carefully*) So she'd no idea how long he'd got?
HEWITT	I can't answer that. Is that why you're haunting this place — you and the inspector?
CLUFF	Mole has a job to do. I'm just a friend of the family.
HEWITT	His car was at the bottom of the hill when I arrived.
CLUFF	Was it?
HEWITT	You didn't notice?
CLUFF	I came over the top, and I'd a load on me mind.

(*A brisk knock at the front door, off* R.)

HEWITT	That'll be him now. (*Slight pause.*) I'll go.

(*He walks out,* DR. CLUFF *paces the room, brooding. Voices in the hall, before* MOLE *comes in followed by* HEWITT.)

MOLE	Cluff! I hardly recognised you without the dog. (*He scans the room.*) Where is it?
CLUFF	It?
MOLE	The dog.
CLUFF	Seen 'em often have you, at funerals and such-like?
MOLE	Er — quite. (*Turns to* HEWITT.) I wonder if you'd excuse us, doctor?
CLUFF	We've nothing to talk about.
MOLE	Indeed we have and I for one would prefer to talk about it in private.

CLUFF	(*as* HEWITT *moves*) Stay where you are, please.
MOLE	Really, Cluff —
CLUFF	Go on, spit it out. You're going to accuse him of issuing a wrong death certificate, aren't you?
MOLE	I wouldn't put it as strongly as that —
CLUFF	I would. Do you deny it?
	(*A moment of unease.*)
HEWITT	Inspector, I've lived in these parts all my life. More than seventy years. Nothing like this has ever been levelled at me before.
MOLE	Anyone can make a mistake, doctor.
CLUFF	You've never owned up to one.
HEWITT	If you'll excuse me, I think I need a breath of clean fresh air. (*He straightens, and walks out into the yard.*)
CLUFF	(*regarding* MOLE *balefully*) What a man's been all his life — that counts for nothing?
MOLE	I am in duty bound to discover the truth.
CLUFF	Aren't we all? I tried to tell you last night, you mean well but you're barking up the wrong tree, as per usual.
MOLE	So there *is* something worth investigating?
CLUFF	I didn't say that.
MOLE	You don't have to. I know that look on your face and I know this boorish attitude, of old. You're on to something.
CLUFF	You go your way, I'll go mine. Agreed?
MOLE	It'll be too late for anyone to go anywhere, once the hearse has been.
CLUFF	No, it won't. Ted's not being cremated, is he?

MOLE   And why — hasn't it struck you? A cremation
            order requires the signature of *two* doctors,
            not just one. Hewitt's been a personal friend
            of theirs as long as you have.

CLUFF   He's been a doctor — and a good 'un — a lot
            longer than that.

MOLE   Why are you being so contrary when you
            know perfectly well —

CLUFF   (*plainly*) These are my fowk. I was born and
            bred amongst 'em. I know 'em — backwards.
            And I don't like foreigners coming here and
            sticking their noses —

MOLE   So I'm a foreigner now? All the way from
            Leeds!

CLUFF   You'd never smelt a blade of grass before
            they sent you here —

MOLE   Make no mistake about it, I've been looking
            for the man responsible ever since!

CLUFF   You've had it easy — all of it. Two fine
            children and a good wife. Doctor Bill lost his
            only son twenty years back — and the woman
            he married's gone now as well. He's alone in
            the world.

MOLE   I'm very sorry. But this happens to be a
            police inquiry and —

CLUFF   Therefore people — as such — don't matter.

MOLE   (*a deep breath*) In view of this recalcitrant
            attitude, I shall get Barker up here as soon as
            possible. (*He crosses to the phone.*)

CLUFF   Good idea. He talks sense — now and again.

MOLE   (*stops, pointing at the phone*) And that's another
            thing — why don't you shout it from the
            house-tops that you won't see her stuck fast?
            This telephone's working now — it was dead
            as a doornail two days ago. Anybody else in

Gunnarshaw would have to wait a month at least to get their phone back. How the devil do you manage it?

(*A slight pause.*)

CLUFF   Connections.

(MOLE *snorts, and turns back to pick up the phone. His finger is on the dial when the laboured sound of* BARKER'S *car is heard, as it draws up outside.*)

MOLE   What's that racket?

CLUFF   Barker's car.

MOLE   Ah! Splendid.

(*He hangs up as* CLUFF *slumps into a chair, aggrieved at this new intrusion on top of* MOLE'S.)

MOLE   (*crossing to* CLUFF) Whichever way you look at it, two days ago a man died all alone in an empty house, with neither wife nor daughter in attendance —

CLUFF   Because neither was expecting him to die.

MOLE   Even if we presume their innocence —

CLUFF   Nay — with you in charge, somebody's bound to be guilty.

(ANNIE CROFT *comes in from the yard, dressed in subdued clothing. She carries a basket containing packages and bulging brown paper bags.*)

ANNIE   Good morning, all.

CLUFF   Speak for yourself. And by the way, that bacon you served up at breakfast was rancid!

ANNIE   (*promptly*) I know! And that was better than you deserved. (*She dumps the basket on the table and starts to unpack it.*)

(SERGEANT BARKER *comes in from outside.*)

CLUFF   And where have you been — sergeant?

BARKER	Making a few routine enquiries.
CLUFF	About what?
BARKER	Ritchie. I've managed to establish there was bad blood between him and Norton.
CLUFF	I could have told you that seven years ago.
MOLE	A poor lookout, if we had to rely on you for information!
CLUFF	Barker's welcome to my old job, as long as he doesn't make a botch of it.
ANNIE	On and on you go, like a pack o' school kids. It gives me a pain just to listen to you.
MOLE	You wouldn't have to, if you hadn't coerced Barker into driving you shopping. He'd have been here long before now.
ANNIE	And what were they coming back to eat — bread and scrape? There's nowt else in the larder.
MOLE	How do you know?
ANNIE	I looked, when I was here last night.
MOLE	(*turns on* BARKER) At least I hope your duties as chauffeur didn't clash with your paid obligations as a policeman?
BARKER	In what way, sir?
	(MOLE *puts a finger to his lips warningly, before he tackles* ANNIE *again.*)
MOLE	Mrs Croft — since you're so conversant with the larder, shouldn't you go and put something in it?
ANNIE	(*her arms full of foodstuffs*) What do you think I'm doing?
CLUFF	No rancid bacon in that lot, is there?
ANNIE	(*glares*) Mind your own business.

(*She sails off* DR. BARKER *closes the door behind her*.)

MOLE   (*ironically*) Now, is there any vague chance that we might get down to brass tacks? Barker, did you manage to make contact with the police surgeon?

BARKER   I did, sir.

MOLE   And?

BARKER   According to him, Norton's symptoms could equally well apply to poisoning.

MOLE   (*to* CLUFF) Did you hear that?

CLUFF   Aye. I wasn't very far away.

MOLE   Go on, Barker.

BARKER   However, without a clinical examination of the stomach's contents —

(CLUFF *clouts the table and rises*.)

CLUFF   Here we go! (*He stumps over to the shelves and takes the mushrooms down*.) If you're trying to tell me Ted couldn't tell a mushroom from a toadstool, you're in the wrong job — both of you.

MOLE   I see! The same thought had occurred to you then?

CLUFF   I should hope so, since these were staring us in the face!

MOLE   And not one single syllable out of you?

CLUFF   Here. (*He shoves the basin at him*.) Try one. (*He goes trundling out*, DR.)

BARKER   There could still be a connection. He knows that. That's why he's walked out.

(*But* MOLE *is gazing thoughtfully down at the basin of mushrooms*.)

MOLE   Norton's stomach. (*Looks up.*) That's my
            trouble too, you know.

BARKER   I'm sorry, Sir.

MOLE   If this place isn't guaranteed to give a man
            ulcers, I don't know what is.

BARKER   (*refers to notebook*) Abdominal pains, vomiting
            — and prostration . . .

MOLE   How revolting! (*Looks at mushrooms again.*)

BARKER   . . . resulting in a fatal coma. And that's how
            Caleb found him.

MOLE   (*murmurs*) All right, Barker.

BARKER   His face was yellow —

MOLE   (*queasy*) Don't go on —

BARKER   — and the features all contorted —

MOLE   That will do! (*He sets the basin aside.*)

            (CLUFF *returns with an official form in his hand,
            which he displays to* MOLE.)

CLUFF   You won't listen to me. P'raps you'll listen to
            that.

            (MOLE *takes it, giving it a glance.*)

MOLE   (*to* BARKER) The death certificate. (*Waving it
            at* CLUFF.) Did she make you a present of
            this, or have you got the run of the whole
            house now?

CLUFF   Wouldn't occur to you, would it? Even the
            Nortons have a family Bible — and that's
            where that 'ud rest till they found time to
            enter the details up.

MOLE   (*eyes to heaven*) Gunnarshaw!

            (*Unobserved,* DR HEWITT *appears in the doorway*
            ULC.)

CLUFF	Go on, take a good look ... it's not infectious.
MOLE	See here, Cluff —
CLUFF	Don't have to, do you? I thought you wouldn't have left the registrar out of your — (*Swings round on* BARKER.) — 'routine enquiries'.
BARKER	(*steadily*) I try to do the job I'm paid for.
CLUFF	(*raps*) Then try harder!
HEWITT	(*coming forward*) He died of heart failure, gentleman, just as it says on the form.
MOLE	Here. (*Handing it back to* CLUFF.) Put this back in the Holy Book. You see, doctor, we're not concerned with the immediate cause of death — it's what led up to it that counts.
HEWITT	I have all the records.
BARKER	It seems mushroom poisoning could have had the same effect. (*Tapping his notebook*.) We've checked the symptoms, doctor.
MOLE	If there's the slightest chance of a mistake, isn't it in your own interests to correct it — while we can?
HEWITT	His heart stopped beating. I recorded the fact. It's as simple as that.
BARKER	But from information received, sir, you'd been treating him for a *liver* complaint.
HEWITT	Exactly so. But one thing leads to another —
MOLE	How true. Now, his last illness and a case of poisoning: couldn't there have been some sort of, well, confusion?
HEWITT	That's possible. Remotely.
MOLE	(*presses his advantage*) Couldn't somebody have been *relying* on it — plus the fact that he'd had similar attacks before?

HEWITT   (*to* BARKER) I take it your information came
              from the police surgeon. Does he agree I
              could have made an error?

MOLE   Careful, Barker —

BARKER   That all depends, sir.

HEWITT   On the degree of my senility?

BARKER   On the results of a possible post-mortem.

MOLE   All we're saying is, it might not have
              occurred to you or Cluff to be suspicious at
              the time.

CLUFF   And therefore this isn't worth the paper it's
              written on? (*He tosses the death certificate on the
              table.*)

BARKER   I'd like to point out, inspector, it was Ritchie
              who gathered the mushrooms —

CLUFF   You reckon he'd commit murder and then
              stick the evidence right under my nose?

MOLE   In view of past circumstances, that might not
              have worried him.

CLUFF   (*looking at him*) Oh, I see. I'd blame Nell,
              because she did the cooking. And blaming
              her, I'd keep my mouth shut. Or does it go
              further than that?

BARKER   Ritchie's in and out of this kitchen all the
              time. He could have mixed in poison with the
              good ones after they'd been peeled, or when
              the pan was on the fire —

CLUFF   And just by coincidence nobody ate any but
              Ted?

BARKER   He told me himself what mushrooms there
              were always went to the invalid —

CLUFF   Give it a rest, Barker. You're making Mole's
              case out for him, can't you see?

HEWITT   Against Nell?

CLUFF   That's what he wants. That's all he's wanted
             from the start. (*He moves away from the group,
             and an embarrassed silence falls.*)

HEWITT   This whole thing's quite absurd. Good
             heavens, you might just as well try and
             convict me!

CLUFF   (*turns*) Don't encourage 'em, doctor.

HEWITT   I mean, there's just as much circumstantial
             evidence where I'm concerned. According to
             you, Ted was alive when you left here to
             telephone me. You say you saw Ritchie on
             the way and told him to come back here. He
             never came.

BARKER   We *think* he didn't —

HEWITT   At least, he wasn't on the premises when I
             arrived. And Caleb hadn't had time to get
             back. I had the place to myself. By the time
             anybody else turned up Norton was dead.
             I'm sure you've considered that possibility as
             well, inspector?

MOLE   I have indeed, but the question of motivation
             defeats me there.

HEWITT   That's honest, at any rate.

BARKER   (*pressing his point*) Ritchie's got more
             motivation than anyone. He's lived off the
             Nortons for years and Ted was sick of it.
             Ritchie had nobody else to turn to if he got
             kicked out. You can see how he pulled it off:
             Norton had been on his back four or five
             days, just the right length of time for this
             kind of poisoning —

CLUFF   Providing the doctor can't recognise a poison
             case when he sees one —

BARKER   Granted ... (*Playing his trump card.*) But why
             didn't Ritchie come down from the moor that
             day when he was told? *Unless he knew Norton
             was going to die?*

MOLE   Good thinking. (*Starts for yard.*) Let's call him
            in and give him —

CLUFF   You won't find him anywhere out there.

HEWITT   I haven't seen him at all this morning —

BARKER   I'll check with Mrs Norton. (*He moves out* DR.)

MOLE   The lad's sure to be here soon. They all plan
            to leave for the funeral together.

CLUFF   Saw the undertaker as well, did you?

MOLE   It's most annoying. Last night, we couldn't
            get him from under our feet!

            (BARKER *returns, with a serious-faced* ANNIE
            beside him.)

BARKER   Mrs Croft's got something to say, sir.

ANNIE   Ritchie's gone: vanished into thin air.

HEWITT   He's what?

ANNIE   He went out on the razzle last night and he
            hasn't been seen since.

CLUFF   Who says?

ANNIE   I got it from Nell. She doesn't think he'll turn
            up now for the ceremony.

MOLE   I've been in this house a solid half-hour.
            Nobody's breathed a word. It's inconceivable!

CLUFF   Happen you'd hear more if you talked less.

ANNIE   He'll be sleeping it off somewhere, that's all it
            is.

            (*Matter-of-factly, she goes to sort more things from
            her basket. But* MOLE *turns on her like a
            prosecuting counsel.*)

MOLE   She kept it to herself all this time — and
            never set foot outside this house to look for
            him?

ANNIE	She went out twice: once down the road, and once over the fields as far as the canal. There wasn't a sign.
BARKER	(*excited now*) It ties in, sir, don't you see? If Ritchie thought we were on to him, he'd be out of this place like a shot.
MOLE	And why should he think that?
BARKER	Me, talking to him about the mushrooms!
HEWITT	You were interested in them as well, Caleb.
MOLE	(*narrowly*) I didn't know you were here last night, doctor?
HEWITT	Nevertheless I was, but not for long.
MOLE	Nobody's bothered to mention that, either!
HEWITT	(*embarrassed*) You'd probably rather discuss this amongst yourselves. So if you'll excuse me ... (*He goes out*, DR.)
MOLE	Most considerate. (*Meaningly.*) Wouldn't you agree, Mrs Croft?
ANNIE	I'd go as well, but then you see — I'm busy.
	(*She clatters a pile of cutlery on to her tin tray, making him jump.*)
CLUFF	Annie's all right where she is. She won't hear owt she doesn't know already.
ANNIE	Not about the Nortons, I can tell you.
CLUFF	(*daring her*) Go on, then. We're flummoxed, Annie. Sort this lot out for us.
ANNIE	(*picks up tray*) If there's any sorting to be done it's high time you set your mind to it — retired or no. But you'll neither do nowt, nor let it alone, will you? Typical, that is — call yourself a detective? (*She marches out*, DR.)
	(*Pause.*)
CLUFF	(*quietly*) No, not any more.

MOLE   This is no time for idle words, it's a time for
              action. (*Striding to the phone.*) I intend to find
              that fellow Ritchie if it takes every man I've
              got. (*Turning around.*) Including the specials!

              (*As he turns back to the phone, it rings. He leaps
              back as though stung. It rings again.*)

MOLE   Barker.

              (BARKER *goes to the phone and picks it up.* NELL
              and KATHLEEN *enter from the hall, now dressed
              in deep mourning. They halt and watch, in
              silence.*)

BARKER   (*into phone*) Daneghyll Farm. Yes, the
              inspector's here — and Mr Cluff. What did
              you . . . (*Stops to listen.*)

MOLE   (*to* CLUFF) Presumably the station.

              (HEWITT *comes in quietly* DR *and stands beside*
              NELL, *taking her hand discreetly.*)

BARKER   I see. Thank you.

              (*He hangs up. The others are poised for revelation
              — all except* CLUFF, *who has wandered back to his
              favourite position by the hearth.*)

MOLE   Well? Private and confidential, was it? For
              your ears only?

BARKER   (*looking at* CLUFF's *back*) No, sir.

MOLE   Then out with it, man!

BARKER   It's Ritchie: they've just pulled him out of the
              canal.

              (*All stare, except* CLUFF.)

MOLE   So much for your bright little theory about
              mushroom poisoning.

NELL   (*startled*) Poisoning?

              (MOLE *turns on her, coldly.*)

MOLE   So much for Ritchie, anyway.

ANNIE   Kathleen!

(She starts forward, but she is too late. KATHLEEN *has crumpled into an untidy heap on the floor.)*

QUICK CURTAIN.

ACT TWO

Scene One

Shortly afterwards.

KATHLEEN *is now in a chair with* NELL *on one side of her and* HEWITT *on the other.* ANNIE *hovers somewhere in the rear.* BARKER *has moved nearer to the hearth, while* MOLE *stands in splendid isolation.* CLUFF *gazes into the fire.*

As the girl starts to recover, NELL *offers her water to drink.*

HEWITT	Coming round ...
NELL	Drink this, Kathleen. Doctor —
HEWITT	She fainted. Nothing serious, but we'd better get her upstairs now.
	(NELL *hands the glass to* ANNIE, *who empties it in the sink upstage.*)
CLUFF	(*moving in*) Let me.
	(*As they make way for him, he bends in to* KATHLEEN *with his arms outstretched.*)
CLUFF	Come on, love —
KATH	(*shrinking back*) No no!
HEWITT	But Kathleen — it's Caleb.
KATH	l don't want him anywhere near me!
	(CLUFF *straightens and moves away.*)
HEWITT	Nell —
	(*He and* NELL *raise the girl and support her out,* DR.)
ANNIE	I don't know what's come over that lass this morning! (*She hurries off* DR *after them.*)
MOLE	(*coming out of his brown study with a noisy expulsion of breath.*) There you are, then! And it's true to say, you never know what's hanging till it drops. There was I, ready to swear it was the mother.

CLUFF	But now it's Kathleen? Just because she fainted, you're accusing her?
MOLE	I wasn't aware that I'd accused anybody as yet. But if that isn't a girl with something on her conscience, my name's not Percy Mole. What do you think, Barker?
BARKER	I'm sorry, but I still say if it wasn't Ritchie it wasn't anybody.
MOLE	Rubbish! All this upset, and Ritchie goes and strolls into the canal of his own accord?
CLUFF	It's happened before.
BARKER	Especially if he'd been drinking —
MOLE	And where, may I ask, would Ritchie get the money to drink himself silly?
CLUFF	(*slowly*) That's just what I've been thinking.
MOLE	How very remarkable! *And* ... ?
BARKER	I'd like to point out, sir —
MOLE	(*with upraised hand*) Not now, Barker. I believe the Oracle is about to reveal all ...
	(*Pause.*)
CLUFF	(*meditatively*) There's no doubt about it ... Ritchie liked his pint.
	(*Pause.* MOLE *turns, wide-eyed.*)
MOLE	Is that it?
CLUFF	From me ... aye.
MOLE	Then may we please get back to the main issue? (*Checks watch, briefly.*) You now have about ten minutes, Cluff, before the undertaker and the rest of them arrive. I'm going to make one final appeal to what is left of your sense of duty. (*Warning.*) We could be dealing with a case of murder here —

CLUFF	Which one are you on about now, Ritchie or Ted?
MOLE	Not even your remaining influence will block a post-mortem on the nephew I'm giving you one last chance with regard to the uncle.
CLUFF	Ritchie clinches it for you, does he?
MOLE	Two deaths in this house in less than three days: that's more than mere coincidence. (*Ticking off on fingers.*) Ritchie died in the canal. And why? Because he knew something. Something he might have told. *If* someone hadn't prevented him.
CLUFF	Don't stop there.
MOLE	I have a duty to perform — it's a word you never recognised. However unpleasant the task, I am determined to save you from yourself —
CLUFF	Spell it out then, shall we? And you can put this down in your little book, Barker, if you've a mind. (*Advancing on* MOLE, *ticking off points on his fingers now.*) Number One, refusal to cooperate in the investigation of a serious crime. Number Two, obstructing the police in the execution of their duty. Number Three, the deliberate concealment of material evidence —
MOLE	When did I say that?
CLUFF	I want Ted Norton buried, don't I? What else would you call it? And having started, let's go the whole hog — Number Four, accessory after the fact ... if not before.
MOLE	(*clenching his fists*) Give me strength!
CLUFF	You're going to need more than that. (*Clouts hand on table, losing his temper.*) Mushrooms and poisoning, my foot! What's wrong with a pillow over Ted's face, while he was lying there unconscious?

(*A beat.*)

BARKER   They'll find that out, if you give them the chance.

CLUFF   Taking any bets, Barker?

BARKER   (*forging ahead*) That way, it could still be Ritchie. If he came back that day when you sent him — suffocated the husband — and then cleared off before the doctor had a chance to get here —

CLUFF   Use your common sense.

MOLE   Wait. I think Barker's hit on something. What if Ritchie *saw it happen*? For all we know, either of the women could have been in this house during that crucial half-hour. If Ritchie did come back, and saw someone — mother or daughter —

CLUFF   Or the other.

MOLE   (*halted in mid-flight*) What other?

CLUFF   The one I mentioned last night, when you were too busy to notice. Suspect Number Four . . . (*He taps his own chest.*)

MOLE   (*gapes*) You!

BARKER   You won't save either of them that way.

CLUFF   (*now dominant*) I was the last person on earth to see Ted alive. I had the means, the motive and the opportunity. And where was I last night when Ritchie went for his midnight swim? You saw nothing of me, either of you, till you came back this morning —

MOLE   Hold on. According to Annie, Nell Norton was out by herself last night, and along by the canal —

BARKER   You see? You can't do it, Caleb not even for her.

CLUFF   You don't know what I can do, lad, when I'm forced. (*He sits, weary and alone.*)

MOLE   Get her back, Barker.

CLUFF   (*as* BARKER *moves*) No! Just listen a minute, the pair of you.

(BARKER *stops in his tracks.* CLUFF *gives them a long hard look, before he resumes.*)

The next thing you'll get on to is law and order — right? You'll remind me yet again that I was once a policeman and that there ought to be a bit o' that left, somewhere inside. (*Grimly.*) Well let me tell you something: that job brought me nowt but turmoil from start to finish. Bobbying's another name for bringing hurt into people s lives, everywhere you go. Now I come from the land: I want to watch things grow, not tear 'em down.

BARKER   (*softly*) Do you know what you're saying?

MOLE   (*softly*) Quiet.

BARKER   Do you know what you're *doing*?

MOLE   (*stronger*) Let him finish!

CLUFF   I never had a farm of me own because Cluff's Head went to my elder brother, and that was only right and proper. (*He leans forward.*) But if I see a chance, even after all these years, of getting something I've always wanted — plus the only woman I ever loved into the bargain — who's going to blame me for taking it? (*He drops his voice.*) Besides — for what it's worth — once upon a time, I was Sergeant Cluff. And nobody in these parts — nobody — would ever suspect Cluff. Least of all, a doctor who'd known him all his life. And even if that doctor did catch on — when it was too late — as like as not he'd hold his peace. He might even try to take the blame himself.

(He lapses into silence. The others look at each other in consternation. A long pause.)

BARKER   I'm sorry Caleb, but that still doesn't explain Ritchie.

CLUFF   Work that out for yourself. It's easy. I'm sorry Ritchie isn't here to help you — but he's where he'll never talk about it now.

(Another pause.)

MOLE   *(slowly)* I think — in all our interests, I should refer this to County Headquarters. *(But he makes no move.)*

CLUFF   *(rising)* I'll save you the trouble. *(He crosses to the phone and dials.)* Detective Chief Superintendent, please; it's personal. *(Pause.)* Cluff. *(MOLE is at his shoulder by now. He reaches over to take the receiver.)*

MOLE   *(meaning it)* Not this way, Caleb.

(He replaces the phone, and they hold each other's gaze.)

CLUFF   Do nothing . . . and I'll marry Nell as soon as it's decent.

BARKER   *(clearly)* Checkmate.

CLUFF   I think he's right. Don't you?

(ANNIE enters DR with an empty tray.)

ANNIE   Still dragging on, is it? *(She closes the door and then pauses, her hand on the knob, sensing something odd.)* What's up with you all?

(CLUFF sits by the hearth.)

Forget I spoke. *(She returns the tray to the table, where she picks up the death certificate.)* What's this doing here? You're not trying to nail Doctor Bill now, are you?

MOLE   Oh, get on with your work, woman.

ANNIE   Don't you call me a woman!

               (MOLE *turns upstage, in a quandary.* ANNIE *puts
               the form on the shelf and moves the mushrooms out
               of her way before unwrapping further bags —
               boiled ham, and the makings of a salad — her
               glance flickering from one to the other of them.*)

ANNIE   I think — between you — you're making a
               right poultice out o' this.

               (MOLE *swings round, then crosses decisively to the
               phone and dials.*)

MOLE   Hello? Is it *really*? From the way you say
               'Gunnarshaw Police Station' anyone might
               think it was the morgue. This is Inspector
               Mole ... Oh, good lord! (*He turns to* BARKER.)
               He's dropped his glasses. (*Into the phone
               again.*) Ah! Back in the land of the living, are
               we? I don't know whether to be glad or sorry.
               Now about Richard Norton —

BARKER   They'll have him at the mortuary, sir, not the
               station —

MOLE   (*ignores this*) That's right, Richard Norton,
               commonly known as 'Ritchie' — and I do
               mean 'common'. Was the police surgeon
               summoned? He was? Incredible. What's his
               initial report? (*Nods sardonically.*) Drowned.
               That's not unusual, when a man's been in the
               canal all night. Anything else? (*Waits.*) You're
               absolutely sure? (*He turns and looks at* CLUFF.)

CLUFF   (*rises*) There wasn't a mark on him, was
               there?

MOLE   (*into phone*) I'll be in touch. (*He hangs up and
               consults his watch.*)

CLUFF   Checking the time won't stop the hearse
               coming.

MOLE

I don't think you and I have anything further to discuss. (*He jams his cap on, walks out, and disappears down the yard.*)

CLUFF

Well, Barker?

BARKER

I'll be back. (*He moves out after* MOLE.)

ANNIE

(*arms akimbo*) Now then, Caleb Cluff —

CLUFF

Don't you start. (*He sits again.*)

ANNIE

Are you going to frame yourself, or what?

CLUFF

I don't mix work with funerals — not as a rule. (*He stretches his legs out in front of him and clasps his hands behind his neck.*)

ANNIE

(*mutters*) You ought to make 'em sorry they started all this. (*She goes back to her chores.*)

CLUFF

Poor old Ted then, eh? They're all going, one by one — the old familiar faces.

ANNIE

Been more than I care to think about lately.

CLUFF

Goes back a long time. First the War ... then Korea ... and after. (*Sighs.*) Alan Hewitt, eh?

ANNIE

The Doctor's son — what about him?

CLUFF

He was another. Bosom pals we were in the old days, over at Cluff's Head.

ANNIE

I remember. (*With a wry look.*) Just.

CLUFF

Grand to be young. Lambing-time ... haying ... shearing. Bonnie lasses, walking up from Gunnarshaw to lend a hand. Us — walking 'em back home again in evening light — (*He quietens.* ANNIE *darts a glance at him, and for once her look is one of sympathy.*)

ANNIE

(*softly*) She wasn't the only pebble on the beach, you know. In those days, you could have had your pick.

CLUFF

You reckon?

ANNIE	But it was always Nell, wasn't it?
CLUFF	Always. Anybody else would have been second best.
ANNIE	And that wouldn't have done for a Cluff.
	(CLUFF *rises suddenly*.)
CLUFF	That's it — why didn't l think of it? — second-best! (*He returns to the mantelpiece*.)
ANNIE	No use asking what you're on about, I suppose? (*Waits*.) I thought not. (*She holds up a crestfallen tomato*.) Does he call that a tomato? I bought these from that pal of yours in the High Street. 'Home Produce', he calls it: who does he deal with, Homes for the Aged?
	(CLUFF *has gone off into a world of his own. She moves nearer, concerned now*.)
	Why do you always have to put yourself through it like this?
CLUFF	(*obliquely*) He'd have made a good doctor — if he'd lived.
ANNIE	Alan Hewitt? (*Shakes her head*.) Too headstrong. Anything Alan wanted he had to grab —
CLUFF	He was only a kid when he died. He'd have grown out o' that.
ANNIE	Choose how, he drove that car of his like a young maniac. I wasn't capped when he had that smash.
CLUFF	Only a bit of a kid ... and kids make mistakes.
	(*The door* DR *clicks and* DR HEWITT *enters, glancing at his pocket-watch on its silver chain*.)
HEWITT	They're very late.
ANNIE	There'll soon be nobody left to go! We've lost Ritchie — and Kathleen's not fit, is she?

HEWITT	(*shakes his head*) I've given her a sedative.
CLUFF	Do you carry 'em about with you?
HEWITT	There were tablets in the house I'd prescribed for Nell. She'll be sound asleep soon.
ANNIE	I'll keep an eye on her till you get back.
HEWITT	(*winding watch*) It isn't like an undertaker to be late.
CLUFF	Especially ours. Time's money, to that old skinflint. I wonder why?
	(HEWITT *is watching* ANNIE'S *preparations, as she busies herself slicing cucumbers*.)
HEWITT	Boiled ham and salad ... tinned fruit. It never varies. And the table all set out in the front parlour.
ANNIE	Well, you have to. Traditional, isn't it?
HEWITT	I wonder how long it is since they ate a meal through there?
CLUFF	Whenever it was, it'd be like dining in church.
HEWITT	Yes. Our front parlours are sacred to the great occasion — births, marriages and deaths. Ted's wedding breakfast, do you think?
ANNIE	Nay, Kathleen's christening came after that.
CLUFF	That's right. I hadn't gone back off leave more than a month. They wrote to me when I was laid up in Korea, and mentioned she'd married him. Kathleen was walking by the time I got back.
ANNIE	(*ruefully*) And no more after her.
HEWITT	These things can't be arranged. It was the same for me.

(*Offstage there is the sound of a heavy engine, labouring up the hill.*)

HEWITT   At last.

(MOLE *returns from the yard, followed by a rather red-faced* BARKER.)

MOLE   (*to* CLUFF) They're here.

ANNIE   (*moves*) I'll warn Nell.

CLUFF   No need. She can hear that engine as well as I can.

BARKER   We did try everything, Caleb, before we —

CLUFF   It's all right, I'm not blaming you. (*He picks up his hat and coat and takes a step towards the yard.*)

ANNIE   Where are you going? They'll come to the front —

CLUFF   I'm not needed now. (*Turns to* MOLE.) Isn't that right, inspector?

BARKER   If you've got any feelings left for Mrs Norton — (*He breaks off as* CLUFF *regards him, stonily.*)

CLUFF   Feelings, lad? Don't you talk to me about feelings.

(CLUFF *starts to pull on his coat.* NELL *enters,* DR. *She has changed out of her funeral clothes into everyday dress, and looks neat and respectable. She wears her second-best coat and carries a hat. She crosses straight to* MOLE.)

NELL   Kathleen's almost asleep. You won't let them disturb her, when they carry him down?

(MOLE *shakes his head soberly.*)

ANNIE   Nell, you're not going dressed like that!

NELL   I know what I'm doing, Annie. (*She goes to the mirror to adjust her hat.*)

CLUFF   I'll leave you all to it then.

MOLE   You can't walk out now! I order you to stay.

CLUFF   (*almost smiling*) Hear that, Barker? You know
              how I feel about orders. (*Glances at* MOLE,
              then back at BARKER.) I've absolutely no right
              to ask you — sergeant — but I'm going to.
              Which is it to be: him, or me? (*He turns on his
              heel and goes.* BARKER *looks round at* MOLE,
              *briefly, and then follows his old boss, closing the
              door softly behind them.*)

MOLE   (*grits*) I'll have that young man back on the
              beat for this!

NELL   (*crossing to him*) I take it you'd like me to
              come to the station with you?

MOLE   Then you've realised —

NELL   Of course. I'd changed my dress before I
              heard the motor.

              (*Awkwardly,* MOLE *takes official-looking
              documents from his pocket.*)

MOLE   I have all the requisite papers —

NELL   (*not looking*) I'm sure you have. You'd never
              have come without them.

HEWITT   Papers — for what?

MOLE   I regret, doctor — that isn't a hearse outside.

ANNIE   But we just heard it arrive —

NELL   Not the hearse, Annie, they must have
              cancelled that. Yes, inspector?

MOLE   I'm afraid so.

NELL   (*to* ANNIE) It's a police van.

MOLE   (*to* HEWITT) And here's my authority for the
              post-mortem on Edward Norton.

HEWITT   Obtained even before you knew Ritchie was
              missing?

MOLE   I had a choice before that of using it or not.
        But once I heard he'd gone ... (*He breaks off
        and shrugs his shoulders, almost apologetically.*)

NELL   You're very certain of yourself, aren't you?

MOLE   In my position, ma'am, I have to be.

        (ANNIE *makes a move for the yard.*)

HEWITT It's no use, Mrs Croft. There's nothing Caleb
        can do now. That's why he left.

ANNIE   But they can't stop the funeral, almost at the
        graveside!

HEWITT Oh yes, they can ... (*At* MOLE.) ... provided
        they have the necessary papers.

NELL   There was never going to be a funeral. Not
        from the moment they started whispering
        down in the town, and word of it got through
        to the police.

ANNIE   (*to* MOLE) He'll pay you out for this, you
        mark my words.

NELL   They all knew I was never in love with Ted.
        Some of them knew what our life was like.
        That's true, isn't it, Mr Mole — I'd far too
        much to gain from my husband's death for it
        to be natural causes?

        (*There is an official knock at the front door, off* R.
        For a second, nobody moves.)

ANNIE   I'd better go and —

NELL   No! This is still my house. (*She turns to*
        MOLE.) Will you show them where the body
        is, or shall I?

MOLE   Stay with her, Mrs Croft. Don't leave her for
        a second. (*Putting his cap on, he goes out* DR.)

        (BLACKOUT.)

Scene Two

That evening.

A dog is barking furiously, offstage.

The daylight is fading now and the kitchen is grey and dull, despite the glow from the fire. NELL *leans forward in the fireside chair, deep in thought. Her coat and hat have gone.*

ANNIE CROFT *rocks herself in the rocker, making its hinges squeak. A sudden gust of wind whips the casement open with a crash, bringing* ANNIE *to her feet, but leaving* NELL *unmoved.* ANNIE *hurries upstage to close it. She has to struggle.*

ANNIE (*strung up*) Isn't that dog ever going to quieten down? It's been ranting and raving on all afternoon. (*No answer. She moves to the door and opens it, peering out.*) I thought at first it might be Caleb's — sounds like his bark. But Clive's too old to kick up a din like that. (*Shivers, closing door.*) This weather. I said this weather! (*There is no reply. She comes down to* NELL's *side.*) High time you had a bite to eat, love.

     (*Pause.*)

NELL He was well rid of me, Annie.

ANNIE Caleb?

NELL Others thought so too.

     (ANNIE *is silent.*)

     (*changing the subject*) How much longer are they going to be? It's ages since they took Ted out of here.

ANNIE I'll stay with you till we know.

     (*The wind blows, the dog keens, and* ANNIE *has nothing further to say. The door opens and, after a brief look inside,* CLUFF *enters and switches on the light. He no longer wears the black tie. The women watch him as he takes off his tweed hat and the old, crumpled Burberry.)*

ANNIE	Cat got your tongue then?
CLUFF	So there's been no word?
ANNIE	Nothing. I thought you'd be going down there to straighten 'em out.
CLUFF	I doubt they'd let me in. I've been at home.
ANNIE	I can see that: you've got pipe-ash all over your tie.
CLUFF	*(brushes it clean)* Can I sit down?
NELL	Do you have to ask, now?
CLUFF	I'm not sure of me welcome, after what I let 'em do.

(NELL goes no further.)

ANNIE	Get sat down. Tea's all gone.

(CLUFF sits in the rocker.)

CLUFF	I'm not surprised, with you on the premises.
NELL	Caleb what are they doing, all this time?
CLUFF	Dr Hewitt's been at it half a century. He doesn't make mistakes. They'll find that out.
NELL	It reflects on him, too. *(Lowers her eyes.)* Everybody. Every single person we ever met ... *(Her voice dies away.)*
CLUFF	*(to ANNIE)* How's Kathleen?
ANNIE	Still asleep when I looked in. Nell didn't want her disturbed.
CLUFF	Go and check.

(ANNIE looks at NELL, whose withdrawn attitude tells her nothing. She looks back at CLUFF who jerks his head, indicating he wants her out. She goes off DR. CLUFF studies NELL, who finally looks up again.)

NELL It's true Caleb, and you know it. Everybody who tries to help the Nortons suffers in the long run.

CLUFF We'll get word soon. The police surgeon can't handle it himself, they have to get an expert in.

NELL Why did it have to turn out like this? I've been sitting here thinking ... looking back. It could have been so good for us, for you and me, but everything had to go wrong.

CLUFF I blame nobody but meself. If only I'd spoken up about how I felt ... but they'd posted me overseas and there was a war on. It wouldn't have been fair to ask anybody to marry me.

NELL I could have waited. *Should* have waited.

CLUFF Should you, Nell?

NELL And to make things worse, when you came back you were wounded. Badly wounded. You'll never know how that made me feel.

CLUFF Never mind, they patched me up, didn't they? (*Thumps his leg.*) Good as new now. (*We realise this is why he takes a walking-stick with him everywhere.*)

NELL Whatever happens, whatever they do to me, I want you to know there's nothing I can remember — before Ted — that doesn't include you.

(*A pause, then* ANNIE *enters* DR.)

ANNIE There's a car pulling up outside.

NELL (*rising quickly*) Is Kathleen awake?

ANNIE (*nods*) Dressing. She'll be down directly.

(*A car door slams, off.*)

CLUFF Let 'em in, Annie, whoever it is.

(ANNIE *leaves* DR, *as he gets to his feet.*)

CLUFF   What's wrong with Kathleen, Nell? You'd better tell me, quick.

NELL   (*agitated*) Nerves, that's all — just nerves ...

CLUFF   Seeing her father dead didn't put her in this state — what's bigger than that?

NELL   Don't ask —

CLUFF   I've got to. (*He takes her by the shoulders.*) What did she find out last night she didn't know before?

NELL   I — I can't tell you.

CLUFF   (*draws her close*) Can't tell me? Not even me ... or me especially?

NELL   (*forcing herself to look at him*) Tell me something first — something I've hoped and prayed for — something that'll make some good come out of it. (*Searching his face.*) Caleb, when all this is finished ... will there be any chance again, for you and me?

(CLUFF'S *expression changes to anger.*)

CLUFF   You could do that? (*He pushes her roughly away from him.*)

(ANNIE *comes back* DR, *and holds the door.*)

ANNIE   I'll give you three guesses.

(MOLE *comes in past her, inwardly contrite and ill-at-ease, outwardly attempting to retain his formal image.*)

MOLE   Still here, Cluff?

CLUFF   Say what you've got to say without the trimmings.

MOLE   Have you any idea where Barker's got to?

CLUFF   I've not seen him since this morning.

MOLE   He left with you —

CLUFF   He didn't come back with me.

ANNIE   (*breaking in*) Can't you tell her then, without
            all this? Don't you know what it *means* to the
            woman?

MOLE   (*to* NELL) Mrs Norton, I came in person
            because I felt I owed it to you. After all, it
            was at my instigation that your
            husband ... that the funeral ... (*At* CLUFF.)
            Not that I was entirely at fault, you
            understand.

CLUFF   It showed nowt, did it? Ted's post-mortem.
            And neither did Ritchie's. Nothing!

MOLE   (*to cover himself*) It'll be some days before the
            tests are complete ...

CLUFF   They'll be negative, and you know it —
            otherwise you wouldn't be here.

            (NELL *is swaying with relief.*)

ANNIE   (*goes to her*) Hear that, love? There's nowt else
            to worry about.

MOLE   She's right. Will you please accept my sincere
            apologies? As a public servant, I am compelled
            at times to courses I cannot avoid —

NELL   You're not alone in that.

CLUFF   Right. When you've all stopped weeping on
            each other's shoulders, can Ted be put away
            now — decently — where he belongs?

MOLE   There's no further objection.

CLUFF   What about Ritchie?

MOLE   We'll take the necessary steps as soon as
            possible.

            (NELL *moves quickly to take a coat down from the
            door.*)

ANNIE   Nell, you ought to tell Kathleen —

            (NELL *glances at her briefly, before hurrying out
            by the yard door.*)

CLUFF   Let her go. She needs to be by herself for a
            bit. But if it's the stock she's worried about,
            all that's been seen to.

ANNIE   It was you round the farm, then? That's what
            the dog was on about. You've been in the
            buildings.

CLUFF   I've got yon shippon mucked out, and the
            milking's all done.

MOLE   Unlike me, then, you haven't been wasting
            your time? (*Sighs heavily.*) I suppose I'll never
            hear the last of this in Gunnarshaw —

CLUFF   Not while I'm about. I'll grant you one thing
            though, you came in person when a phone-
            call would have done. Ten out o' ten for that.

MOLE   There's an end of it then. (*Magnanimously.*)
            Cluff, I am closing the file.

CLUFF   That's good ... 'cos I'm just opening mine.

            (*A pause, as* MOLE *grits his teeth.*)

MOLE   I ask myself time and again, all through my
            sleepless nights — what did I ever do to get
            posted here?

CLUFF   I've been studying things out you see, just to
            keep me hand in.

MOLE   It's asking the impossible, I know, but may I
            be told the reason for this complete *volte-face*?

CLUFF   It's Ritchie. See?

MOLE   No, as usual I do not see.

CLUFF   Walked into the canal of his own accord, did
            he? Just to round everything off nicely?

MOLE   That's what you've been claiming all day —

CLUFF   Not me. Barker.

MOLE   And I agree with him, finally. Ritchie
            couldn't have known anything about his
            uncle's death because there was nothing at all
            to know. So why should anyone want to do
            away with him?

CLUFF   That's straightforward enough. It's a pity Life
            never seems to be.

            (MOLE *turns to* ANNIE *for support.*)

ANNIE   Don't look at me. I've been trying for
            donkeys years — I'll never fathom him.

MOLE   (*turning back to* CLUFF) Haven't I bent over
            backwards to prove your point? Backwards!
            Norton died for exactly the reason your
            doctor friend said he did —

CLUFF   I know.

MOLE   And now the foremost forensic scientist in
            the North of England bears you out —

CLUFF   I know that as well.

MOLE   I give up. I simply give up! (*He collapses into
            the rocking-chair.*)

ANNIE   (*helpfully*) Drink o' water, Mr Mole?

MOLE   Nothing short of hemlock would meet the
            case. For the first time in my life Mrs Croft, I
            am completely lost for words.

            (*At the yard door, the sneck is lifted from outside.*)

ANNIE   We've got company.

            (BARKER *comes in from the yard.*)

CLUFF   You've taken your time. I could have walked
            to Halifax and back by now.

BARKER   The car broke down.

CLUFF	(*sadly*) Again?
BARKER	And I'd a lot of people to see.
MOLE	(*suspiciously*) On your behalf, or Cluff's?
ANNIE	It's all over and done with. (*Points at* MOLE.) He's just been saying —
MOLE	From the amount of alcohol in Ritchie's stomach, he couldn't have found his way home in broad daylight, let alone traverse a narrow tow-path on a pitch-black night. Death by misadventure.
CLUFF	That won't do for Barker. It won't do for me. And it certainly won't do for Gunnarshaw.
MOLE	Just what have you and Barker been up to?
CLUFF	You might say I've been assisting the police in their enquiries. The right and proper ones this time.
MOLE	Assisting? You?
CLUFF	Anyway, I thought you'd finished talking — can't somebody else have a go? (*As* MOLE's *eyes pop*.) Your turn, Barker.
BARKER	(*with notebook out*) Ritchie called at a pub on his way in last night —
CLUFF	Only one?
BARKER	Several others, later on; but there's a gap of one solid hour in between.
CLUFF	Now then, where was he for that solid hour? It's a small market-town, with nothing to brag about in the way of night-life — that's if you don't count a couple of Indian restaurants and a Chinese take-away.
BARKER	I've done the rounds — (*Ruefully*.) — on foot.
CLUFF	(*without sympathy*) Hard luck.

MOLE   You're *making* work now! There isn't a mark
            on Ritchie there shouldn't be. He's been
            written off.

CLUFF   By you, certainly. (*He has his back to* DR, *and
            does not notice* KATHLEEN, *as she comes in. She
            has dressed in a hurry and is keyed up.*)

CLUFF   But you said it first, remember. Two men
            from this farm died within two days of each
            other —

ANNIE   Kathleen —

            (CLUFF *breaks off, turning.*)

KATH   Two men: the one my mother married, and
            his rotten nephew.

MOLE   It's all over, Miss Norton. Everyone's been
            cleared.

KATH   (*straight at* CLUFF) Two men died. Because
            you loved her once. Or pretended to.

ANNIE   Pretended?

KATH   Where is she? They took Ted Norton's body
            out of here — did they take her, too?

CLUFF   Nobody's taken your mother anywhere.

KATH   Not that you'd care. (*Swings round to* MOLE.)
            It's somebody else they should have taken.
            My father. Not the man who used to call
            himself that! Where is she? (*She runs off*, DR.)

ANNIE   (*to* CLUFF) What's the matter with her? She's
            run to you ever since she was a baby —

BARKER   Hysterical — doesn't know what she's saying
            —

MOLE   'Ted Norton'. Is that any way to refer to her
            own father? Though come to think of it, she
            doesn't look much like him.

ANNIE   She favours her mother's side and always did.

MOLE   There's something, somewhere. That death
              certificate, Cluff. You knew exactly where to
              lay your hands on it. (*Rising.*) The family
              Bible, didn't you say — in the front parlour?

              (CLUFF *merely stares at him.*)

              Even I should be able to find that without a
              guide. (*He stalks out* DR.)

CLUFF   He gets there in the end, does Mole.
              Provided you point him in the right direction
              and give him a big shove.

BARKER   He's chasing moonbeams, if you ask me.

CLUFF   Maybe, maybe not. It's set Annie thinking, if
              nowt else!

ANNIE   All too long ago. It mists over in me mind.

CLUFF   But that spring was famous Annie, don't you
              remember? Alan Hewitt killing himself in a
              car-crash, the shock of it giving his mother a
              breakdown. Nell marrying Ted Norton out of
              the blue — Nell's father poorly and sickening
              for worse —

ANNIE   And you weren't here for any of it.

CLUFF   I couldn't be. I was under orders.

ANNIE   Aye. Out in Korea, trying to be a marine
              commando.

CLUFF   I should have been here, though. (*Steadily.*)
              By God, I should have been. (*He goes again to
              the fire, leaving them to draw their own
              conclusions.*)

ANNIE   (*tentatively*) David, what's he getting at?

              (MOLE *comes back in, carrying the Norton's Bible
              — a large old volume with its brass clasp undone.
              He places it on the table near* BARKER.)

MOLE   Let's see if you're as intelligent as Cluff
              makes out. (*As* BARKER *stares at him.*) Open it,
              man — open it at the fly-leaf. Read what's
              there.

BARKER   Sir?

MOLE   Here. (*He flips the front cover open, and taps the
              fly-leaf.*) Births, marriages and deaths — the
              family record, going back over a hundred
              years. It's customary in these parts, you ask
              Cluff — and then tell your former idol where
              it stops short.

CLUFF   You needn't bother.

BARKER   (*looks*) The last entry seems to be Norton's
              marriage.

MOLE   Precisely! And what we want to know is: after
              her recent exhibition does Kathleen Norton
              qualify for inclusion or does she not?

BARKER   Qualify?

MOLE   Is she Norton's flesh and blood, or isn't she?

ANNIE   You what?

CLUFF   Tell him, Annie. Norton never had a chance
              with Nell, for all the sheep's eyes he used to
              cast at her. (*Crossing in.*) How long was it
              after I'd gone back she up and married him?

BARKER   'Pretend'. The girl said you'd pretended —

CLUFF   And how long after that was Kathleen born?

ANNIE   She was a first child —

CLUFF   An *only* child. But was that Nell's fault — or
              Ted Norton's?

              (MOLE *is watching, narrowly.*)

              How long after I went back off embarkation
              leave — come on, Annie — seven months?

ANNIE	A first child — they don't always go full term —
CLUFF	This one did. And I know her birthday, lass, as well as I know my own.
	(*They gaze at him, flabbergasted.*)
	What's the matter? Think I'm incapable, or summat?
MOLE	Never in all my born days —
CLUFF	I daresay not. But I wasn't always as decrepit as I am now. So you can all put that in your pipe and smoke it! (*He stumps off into the yard.*)
MOLE	(*sinking back into his chair*) Cluff's daughter? It's not possible.
ANNIE	He means it. More than he ever meant anything.
BARKER	But he'd never let anybody down like that, it isn't in him!
ANNIE	He was thousands of miles away when the girl was born.
BARKER	Once he came back, he'd set it right.
ANNIE	By then, Nell was Mrs Norton.
MOLE	This explains everything.
BARKER	(*dryly*) Again?
ANNIE	(*turning*) Young Kathleen must be out of her mind with it all. (*She goes off* DR *to see to her.*)
MOLE	If the girl found out after all these years, she'd be capable of anything.
BARKER	I still can't credit it.
MOLE	(*on his feet*) And now she stands condemned, out of Cluff's own mouth.
BARKER	How?

MOLE   Who said something this morning about a
            pillow being pressed over the face —
            suffocation? And Norton must have been as
            weak as a kitten. Even a young girl —

BARKER   So it was Kathleen?

MOLE   All along.

BARKER   But *why*? After all this time?

MOLE   Norton must have known about her. Now if
            for some reason he threatened to make that
            public —

BARKER   What reason, after keeping it dark so long?

MOLE   If he knew he was dying and blamed them
            for the mess he'd made of things —

BARKER   That wasn't Kathleen's fault.

MOLE   Blamed the mother then, in front of her: and
            so it all came out. Oh, it's as clear as crystal
            now! Look how she's behaved since we
            turned up — the way she fainted when —

BARKER   That's where it falls down. If she was clever
            enough to plan all this, and had the nerve to
            carry it through —

MOLE   She thought we'd come for Mrs Norton, and
            that caught her by surprise. Could she let her
            own mother be taken in for something she
            had done?

BARKER   (*a new thought*) Mrs Norton!

MOLE   (*wearing his Sunday face*) The innocent party,
            and a woman much maligned.

BARKER   I wonder. Because everything you've said
            applies to her. And she told you herself she
            stood to gain by her husband's death —

MOLE   But remember the way Kathleen's been
            acting all along — nothing but a bundle of
            nerves.

BARKER	Wouldn't you be? If you thought your own mother had committed murder?

(DR HEWITT *passes the window*.)

MOLE	(*hissing*) That's enough.

(HEWITT *appears in the doorway. He has changed into more everyday attire. Seeing them, he halts and smiles*.)

HEWITT	You've beaten me to it. I'd hoped to be the first.

(CLUFF *walks in after him*.)

CLUFF	Hello, Doctor.
HEWITT	Caleb.
CLUFF	One thing about this farm being perched halfway up a hill, you can see who's coming a mile off.
HEWITT	Have they told you? The first results are out, and the inspector's more than satisfied.
CLUFF	That was an hour ago. He's changed his mind since then.

(HEWITT'S *smile changes to a puzzled frown*. NELL *enters* ULC.)

	Somebody else saw you coming, doctor.
NELL	I'd hoped you'd stay quietly at home.
HEWITT	How could I? They've told you then?
NELL	They've told me. (*She looks at the stern faces of the policemen*.) But that doesn't seem to be the last of it.
MOLE	Barker, I want that girl in.
CLUFF	Not yet. We'll get this little lot sorted first. (*He crosses to take down from the shelves the cocoa-tin that* NELL *uses for household cash. He uncaps it*.)

MOLE	He's not going to make us all a cup of cocoa?!
CLUFF	Empty. But it wasn't empty last night, when you put that change away.
NELL	I owed Ritchie wages.
CLUFF	A bit on account, you might say?
NELL	I'd no more cash in the house.
CLUFF	Inspector, you've seen Ritchie. Any money on him when they pulled him out?
MOLE	Not a penny. You don't think he'd stop drinking while there was any left?
CLUFF	(*turning back to* NELL) He must have made it go a mighty long way.
NELL	You've no idea how much was in there —
CLUFF	Oh yes, I have: I saw it.
NELL	(*not at once*) Kathleen's been down, hasn't she? What's she been telling you?
CLUFF	Enough.
NELL	The man and the policeman ... they'll always be one and the same.
CLUFF	That can't be helped. Listen, all of you. Go back to last night. Ritchie looked to me then like a man with a load off his mind, like someone who was taking over. But taking over what, Nell? Kathleen? The farm? I know he had a weather eye on both.

(*Voices are raised, off in the hall* DR. KATHLEEN, *escaping from* ANNIE, *bursts in.*) |
| KATH | It's no good, I've got to tell them! |
| ANNIE | (*following*) She slipped me. There was no holding her — |

KATH	What's the matter with you all, haven't you got eyes? This house is built into the side of the hill and my bedroom's at the back. All I have to do to get out is step over the window-sill on to the ground —
NELL	Don't listen to her.
KATH	You can't stop me — nobody can!
NELL	She never went out last night, I locked her in.
KATH	Only the door the window locks on the inside.
CLUFF	And you knew the way Ritchie would come back. One strong heave — then back home, the same way?
HEWITT	(*startled*) Caleb, I thought you were their friend —
CLUFF	I'm everybody's friend, for just as long as it suits 'em. After that I'm not fit for 'em to wipe their shoes on. I can forgive crime — sometimes. (*Looking directly at* NELL.) But what I can't stand — and never could — is lies and deceit!
NELL	It's Kathleen who's lying! I knew Ritchie would be drunk and I knew the way he'd come back, the way he *always* came —
KATH	Nobody could hate him the way I did —
NELL	(*topping her*) He knew, Kathleen — *he knew*! (*She turns away, her chest heaving.*)
CLUFF	Take your pick, Inspector. Which is it? Which one of 'em murdered Ted and then killed Ritchie to keep his mouth shut?
HEWITT	This is monstrous. What reason could they have?
CLUFF	Nell?

NELL   (*turns*) Nearly a quarter of a century with Ted
              Norton. Day in, day out. Nothing but
              violence and hatred.

MOLE   More than that. (*He takes a step towards the
              Bible.*)

CLUFF   Not yet, Inspector. We're not there yet.

              (MOLE *returns to his place.*)

KATH   (*soft and intense*) You might stop him, but you
              can't stop me. I'll tell it all in open court —

CLUFF   Your mother's the one to talk, when she's so
              minded.

NELL   Kathleen — if I mean anything at all to you,
              don't go on with this.

              (KATHLEEN *stares for a moment, agonised.*)

KATH   They don't deserve it. Any of them.
              Especially him. (*She buries her face against her
              mother.* NELL *looks round at all of them.*)

NELL   (*steadily*) I came down from the moors that
              day, and Ritchie saw what I did. He was
              going to blackmail me. I couldn't let a man
              like that stay alive.

HEWITT   (*quickly, to* MOLE) You'll never prove a word
              of this in court. A jury will never accept it —

CLUFF   Annie! Get their hats and coats.

ANNIE   What for?

CLUFF   Barker's taking 'em in. (*To* BARKER.) Right,
              Barker?

              (BARKER *stares at him, and then he nods.*)

BARKER   Right. For questioning.

CLUFF   Good lad.

BARKER   (*to* MOLE) If I could use your car, sir, I'll
              drive them into Gunnarshaw.

MOLE   Of course.

                (*He hands his car keys over, as* NELL *and*
                KATHLEEN *turn for the door.*)

CLUFF   Go with 'em, Annie.

NELL   We won't run away ... at least allow us to
                tidy up. (*She takes her daughter out.*)

ANNIE   Fowk don't change, Caleb Cluff. You
                shouldn't have to be told.

CLUFF   I said go with 'em.

                (ANNIE *follows them out, sadly.*)

HEWITT   You honestly think this makes sense, Caleb?

CLUFF   (*slowly*) Can you do any better?

HEWITT   I know how Ted died. So does the Home
                Office pathologist. Nothing can alter the
                post-mortem findings —

CLUFF   I wouldn't want it to. (*He glances at the door.*)
                They should be out of earshot now. Right
                Barker, fetch it over.

                (BARKER *hesitates — and then a light dawns. He
                brings the Bible to* CLUFF.)

                Show it to the doctor. Open.

                (BARKER *lays the Bible in front of* HEWITT, *open
                at the fly-leaf.*)

                Owt strike you about that? The inspector
                tumbled to it straightaway.

HEWITT   I don't see what —

CLUFF   If you don't want to look, we'll tell you who
                Kathleen's real father is.

                (HEWITT'S *head snaps up. Then, without glancing
                at it, he closes the Bible and hands it over to*
                CLUFF, *moving to the fire with his back turned on
                them all.* CLUFF *looks warningly at the other two
                and then crosses to join him, the Bible under his
                arm.*)

CLUFF   A man couldn't hold his head up if it ever
           came out.

HEWITT   I thought better of you than this.

CLUFF   Funny thing, everybody round here knows
           me better than I know myself!

HEWITT   You're determined to go through with it?

CLUFF   I have to. Nobody's bigger than the law. Not
           even you.

           (ANNIE *comes back*, DR.)

ANNIE   They're ready and waiting.

CLUFF   Call 'em in.

ANNIE   (*calling them in*) Nell ... Kathleen —

           (*The two women return, now wearing their coats
           and hats.* CLUFF'S *eyes have never left* HEWITT.)

HEWITT   Hoping she wouldn't be convicted — wasn't
           enough?

CLUFF   It has to be out in the open, doctor.
           Kathleen's got to be certain, once and for all,
           about her mother.

           (*A pause, then* HEWITT *nods briefly*.)

HEWITT   Please tell her, Nell. Whenever you like. (*He
           walks towards the yard.*)

CLUFF   (*sharply*) Haven't you forgotten something?

           (HEWITT *stops and turns. His voice is very quiet.*)

HEWITT   I knew his movements of old. I waited for
           him in the dark.

CLUFF   Thank you, doctor. I take it you'd prefer to
           walk back in?

HEWITT   (*his gentle smile returns*) Trust you to think of
           that. You know where I'll be, Mr Barker. (*He
           walks out with dignity.*)

MOLE	A very touching little display. Will someone kindly tell me what it meant?
BARKER	You'll find out from his statement, sir.
MOLE	Then you understand all this, Barker?
BARKER	I think I'm beginning to.
MOLE	And you've let a man go, in possession of vital information?
BARKER	He'll be waiting for us at the station.
CLUFF	You can bank on that. Tell it now, Nell. It's time, lass.

(NELL *turns to* KATHLEEN.)

NELL	You're his grand-daughter, Kathleen.
KATH	(*amazed*) Doctor Bill's?
ANNIE	Alan Hewitt!
NELL	Yes.
ANNIE	(*to* CLUFF) And you've had us all believing —
KATH	(*goes to him*) Had *me* believing ...
MOLE	Why, Cluff? Why on earth did you try and sacrifice —
CLUFF	Because that would have solved everything. But it wasn't right, and so it didn't work. End of statement.
BARKER	What you're telling us is the doctor's guilty? That he killed them both?
CLUFF	(*shakes his head*) Only Ritchie.
MOLE	Barker, my car keys. At once.

(BARKER *looks at* CLUFF.)

CLUFF	He'll not want company, inspector. And Gunnarshaw would never forgive you for an open arrest.

MOLE   You've never heard of flight, I suppose, let
            alone suicide?

CLUFF   If he'd wanted that way out, he'd have taken
            it long ago.

MOLE   I only wish I had your simple faith. (*He
            rounds on* BARKER.) Do I get those keys or
            don't I?

CLUFF   Give 'em to him Barker, otherwise he'll have
            a stroke.

            (*Reluctantly,* BARKER *hands them over.*)

MOLE   And as soon as you get back to the office, I
            want a long and serious talk with you.

BARKER   I thought you might, sir.

            (MOLE *marches* DR.)

MOLE   You may be right Cluff, and Gunnarshaw
            may never forgive me. But one thing is
            certain — (*Swinging round.*) — *I shall never
            forgive Gunnarshaw!* (MOLE *exits.*)

CLUFF   Check on him. See he goes by road, and then
            come back.

            (BARKER *nods, and follows* MOLE *out.*)

            The doctor's bound to go across the fields.
            He loves this countryside as much as I do.

            (*He is looking at* NELL, *as the front door slams off*
            R.)

NELL   I've no excuses.

CLUFF   For Alan? You don't need any.

NELL   You had to be away so much. I knew you
            loved me, but you'd never mentioned
            marriage. And you were always so — remote.
            When Alan came home from his
            studies ... (*Faltering.*) It's no good, I'll never
            know just how or why it happened —

ANNIE	He could have charmed the devil himself, that one.
CLUFF	But he'd have stood by you, if he'd lived. Alan Hewitt had the right stuff in him. Kathleen — how did you find out Ted wasn't your real father?
KATH	From Ritchie.
NELL	And he said Caleb was?
KATH	He didn't name names. It was me. I jumped to conclusions.
NELL	(*softly*) You see, I knew Kathleen was coming when I got married. Ted wanted me very much. I told him whose child it was — but Alan was dead, and we thought it might just work. We were both wrong.
CLUFF	What made him let it out to Ritchie?
NELL	At the end, he wasn't himself. He seemed — obsessed with failure. I think he broke our secret to give Ritchie a hold over us, because he wanted this farm to stay on in his name. That was the only thing that Ted could leave behind . . . (*She silences.*)
KATH	(*very softly*) Uncle Caleb . . .
CLUFF	Hello! (*Pause.*) That's a start, anyway.
KATH	I feel so ashamed. (*Her head droops.*)
CLUFF	Leave it. Just as long as we're pals again. (*He goes for his hat and coat.*)
ANNIE	Come with me, love.
	(KATHLEEN *looks at* NELL, *then at* CLUFF. *She understands. She goes out quietly, with* ANNIE'S *arm round her shoulders.*)
CLUFF	So the doctor knew it all, from the beginning.

NELL He lived on his memories. All these years, he had his son's reputation to consider, and the memory of his wife. Now he's had to kill — twice — to protect the past.

CLUFF Nobody killed your husband. They made sure of that at the mortuary, and I was never in doubt. (*He pulls on his old raincoat, and starts to button it up.*)

NELL And Ritchie?

CLUFF Ritchie was a different kettle of fish. Once he knew about Kathleen, he'd try to make capital out of it. I saw the mood he was in last night, when he followed the doctor out of here. He must have talked to him and made some sort of proposition. Then, if he was told to call in at the surgery later on, he must have been there for one hour that's not accounted for in his movements. The doctor's surgery. That's where he got his money for booze, and that's when Doctor Hewitt knew it wouldn't be the final payment.

NELL They said there was nothing on him when they dragged him out of the canal —

CLUFF They'll find traces at the doctor's home. He'd have to go in after the lad, to make sure he stayed under.

NELL It's terrible to think of —

CLUFF Maybe, but he wasn't doing it for himself. (*He collects his hat and stick, as* NELL *crosses slowly to the fire.*)

NELL And it all started with talk. I'd have thought that wouldn't count, with you.

CLUFF Only one thing counted, from the very beginning.

(*She turns to face him.*)

CLUFF   I lost my temper with you earlier on. I'm
              sorry. Only it seemed to me that you were
              trying to strike a bargain. Selling yourself,
              body and soul, for your daughter.

NELL   I was. But that wasn't the whole of it.

              (*He takes a quick step towards her, but she shakes
              her head at him sadly.*)

              No, Caleb. Not now. Not ever — for us.
              Thanks to me, it will always be too late.

              (*A pause, as* CLUFF *studies her.*)

CLUFF   Ah, well. I suppose I — I wouldn't wish a
              Sergeant Cluff on anybody, not twenty four
              hours a day ...

              (*There is a thud, a scuffling and an eager whine
              at the yard door. The latch is fumbled open and*
              BARKER *comes in with* CLIVE, *a piece of old cord
              tied to the dog's collar.*)

BARKER   Mole's gone, and he went by road.

CLUFF   How did you manage it?

BARKER   (*laughs*) He said he had to call in home, for a
              dozen aspirin.

CLUFF   Let the dog loose.

              (BARKER *releases* CLIVE. *The dog goes straight to*
              CLUFF, *who undoes the rope.*)

BARKER   I found him tied to a gate-in the bottom
              yard.

CLUFF   And he's been telling the world about it ever
              since.

NELL   Being tied up doesn't agree with him, does
              it?

CLUFF   It never did.

BARKER   I think that runs in the family.

              (NELL *glances at him, thoughtfully.*)

CLUFF   Before you go back for your telling-off, come over to the cottage. We'll have a pint of real ale.

BARKER   Now you're talking!

(CLUFF *turns to look piercingly at* NELL. *It is a kind of good-bye.* NELL *knows, and her eyes are misted.*)

CLUFF   Memories, eh? I daresay they're better than nothing. (*Pats his dog.*) Come on, lad.

(*He and the dog go out together.*)

BARKER   'Night, Mrs Norton.

NELL   (*a world away*) Goodnight, Mr Barker.

(BARKER *goes too, and her eyes stay on the yard door as it closes behind them.*)

ANNIE   (*bustling in again,* DR) Kath wants to know if she can come back now.

NELL   Of course. (*She starts to take her coat off.*) Call her down.

(*Outside, as he romps away, the excited bark of the collie-dog is heard.*)

ANNIE   (*turns at door*) I see that dog's still at it! (*Listens.*) But he sounds more suited, somehow.

NELL   It's Caleb's.

ANNIE   If I didn't think so . . .

NELL   (*slowly*) He's been fastened up a long time. Now he's free.

ANNIE   And that's how it was meant to be.

NELL   Perhaps. (*She puts her coat down, and somehow forces a smile.*) Let's put the kettle on.

ANNIE   (*calling radiantly down the hall*) Come on,
                 Kathleen —— tea up! (*She is crossing to lend
                 a hand, as . . .*)

                 THE CURTAIN FALLS